One-Page COMPOSER BIOS

50 Reproducible Biographies of Famous Composers

Jay Althouse

ISBN-10: 0-7390-6166-6
ISBN-13: 978-0-7390-6166-4

Alfred Music Publishing
16320 Roscoe Blvd., Suite 100
P.O. Box 10003
Van Nuys, CA 91410-0003
alfred.com

Contents

Introduction

One Page Composer Bios is designed to introduce to students the lives of fifty great composers. It may be used, either as supplementary material or as a specific curriculum, in a general music class or in a course in music history. It may also be used as a home school course of study.

The purchaser of this book is granted the right to photocopy the book. Every page may be reproduced in quantity for distribution to students. Students may file the pages or keep them in a binder. At the end of the course of study, the student will have a complete photocopied text-book containing biographies of fifty composers.

Each biography is printed on a single page. The biography focuses on the personal as well as the musical events in the composer's life. It is intended to make the composer more human and personal to students who may think of composers as nothing more than long dead icons.

Also included on each biography page are:

- A portrait
- The composer's dates of birth and death
- A phonetic pronunciation of the composer's name
- The musical era in which the composer lived
- A list of the composer's most famous works
- A quote by or about the composer

Following the fifty composer biographies are six one-page essays on the eras of music.

Johann Sebastian Bach

Yoh'-hahn Sih-bahs'-tian Bahk
(There is no English equivalent for the "ch.")

born March 21, 1685, Eisenach, Germany
died July 28, 1750, Leipzig, Germany

A Composer of the Baroque Era

Both of Johann Sebastian Bach's parents died before he turned ten. After their deaths, Johann lived with his older brother Christoph, a church organist, who taught Johann harpsichord and organ. For most of his life, Johann Sebastian Bach was a church musician, beginning as a boy soprano in a church choir. After his voice changed, he became a violinist in a church orchestra at Lünenberg, near Hamburg, Germany.

As a teenager, Bach often traveled to Hamburg to hear concerts and to take organ lessons. In 1703 (age eighteen), he became the town organist at Arnstadt, and it was here that he first began to compose music. Four years later he married, and was soon appointed the court organist and violinist to the Duke of Weimar. In this position, Bach was able to study all styles of music and develop his composing skills. He wrote many pieces for organ and harpsichord as well as several sacred cantatas.

In 1717, the Prince of Cöthen hired Bach as his court choirmaster. In this position he had more time to compose hundreds of works for clavier (a type of keyboard instrument like a piano), string orchestras, instrumental groups of all sizes, solos, duets, trios, and concertos. His wife, Maria, died suddenly in 1720, and a year later he married Anna Wülken, a fine singer.

Bach remained at Cöthen until 1723 (age thirty-eight), when the Prince's new wife decided she preferred less serious music than that which Bach composed. Bach moved to Leipzig, Germany, and became choirmaster at a private choir school. He also supervised the music in two Leipzig churches and wrote music for all church occasions. Bach was never totally happy in this position, but he took the job so his children could be educated at the school. When he was a court musician, professional musicians were available to perform his music. Here his music was performed, often poorly, by student and amateur musicians. His pay was less and his living conditions were sub-standard. Nevertheless, Bach remained at the choir school for the rest of his life.

In Leipzig, Bach composed almost endlessly, providing music for both the church and the community. He also taught music, Latin, and conducted the choir at the choir school. Occasionally, he traveled throughout Europe to hear the music of other composers.

In appearance, Bach was a bit overweight. He was courteous, dignified, and loyal to his friends. As a teacher, he was considerate and patient with his students. As a composer, he approached his work as a job that had to be done. When asked to describe his life as a composer, he answered, "I worked hard." He wrote in all musical forms and styles except opera. Bach probably would not have expected his music to be performed today, more than 250 years after his death; his goal was simply to create music for everyday occasions in eighteenth century Leipzig.

Famous Works:

Brandenburg Concertos No. 1–6 — for orchestra
The Well-Tempered Clavier — for keyboard
The Art of the Fugue — for organ
St. Matthew Passion — for chorus and orchestra
Mass in B Minor — for chorus and orchestra

"The aim and final end of all music should be none other than the glory of God and the refreshment of the soul."

Johann Sebastian Bach

Béla Bartók

Bay'-la Bar'-tock

Born March 25, 1881, Nagyszentmiklós, Hungary
died September 26, 1945, New York, New York

A Composer of the Twentieth Century

As a child, Béla Bartók took piano lessons from his mother. When Béla was eight, his father died, and at age thirteen he and his mother moved to Pressburg, which is now the capital of Slovakia. Here Béla continued his piano studies, and began to study music theory. After finishing his public schooling, Béla enrolled at the Royal Academy of Music in Budapest, Hungary. By 1903, when he graduated from the Academy, Béla was an accomplished pianist and a talented young composer.

In Budapest, Béla became friends with Zoltán Kodály, a composer who was interested in folk music. Together Béla and Zoltán traveled throughout Hungary collecting folk songs, which they published in a collection in 1906. In 1907, Bartók became a professor of music at the Royal Academy of Music in Budapest. He maintained his interest in folk music and traveled extensively throughout eastern Europe collecting songs. He also arranged many of the folk songs for solo voice and piano.

In 1909 (age twenty-eight), Bartók married Márta Ziegler, and they had a son a year later. Bartók's compositions were not very popular in his native Hungary during this period. His music was very rhythmic and often influenced by the folk songs which he collected. However, a ballet for which he composed the music, *The Wooden Prince,* became popular with Hungarian audiences. This encouraged Bartók, and gave him some recognition within Hungary. Although he still maintained an interest in folk music, he began concentrating more on composing.

After World War I, Bartók began touring as a concert pianist, frequently performing his own compositions. He divorced Márta in 1923 and married one of his piano students. Bartók traveled to the United States in 1927 (age forty-six) for a ten week concert tour sponsored by the Baldwin Piano Company. The concerts received a pleasant, but not overwhelming response. In fact, that was the typical reaction to Bartók's music during his lifetime, both in Hungary and wherever he toured.

Bartók remained on the faculty of the Royal Academy of Music in Budapest until 1934 (age fifty-three) when he resigned to continue his work collecting and arranging folk music. When World War II broke out in Europe, Bartók moved to the United States. By this time, his health was failing, his music was rarely performed, and there was no demand for his skills as a pianist. He died in New York City five years later.

Because of his interest in collecting folk music Béla Bartók has always been recognized as an expert in the field of ethnomusicology, the study of the social and cultural aspects of music. In fact, he is recognized as one of the foremost ethnomusicologists of the twentieth century. His compositions were rarely well received during his lifetime. Today, however, Bartók's rhythmic and folk-influenced compositions are very popular with concertgoers and performers. His six string quartets, which were written over a period of thirty-one years, are highly regarded, and his piano music remains a part of the repertoire for concert pianists.

Famous Works:

His six string quartets — for two violins, viola, and cello
Music for Strings, Percussion and Celesta — for chamber orchestra
Concerto for Orchestra — an orchestral work
Mikrokosmos — for piano
The Wooden Prince — a ballet

"Folk melodies are a real model of the highest artistic perfection."
Béla Bartók

Ludwig van Beethoven

Lood'-vig fahn Bay'-toh-vn

born December 16, 1770, Bonn, Germany
died March 26, 1827, Vienna, Austria

A Composer of the Classical and Romantic Eras

Ludwig van Beethoven had a very poor and unhappy childhood. He began piano lessons at age four. When Ludwig turned eight, his father decided to make money from his son's talent. He presented Ludwig as a concert pianist and advertised that the eight year old Ludwig was only six years old.

Although Ludwig was never a successful child performer, as his father had hoped, by fourteen he was quite a good musician and became the assistant organist at a local church. At seventeen, he met composer Wolfgang Amadeus Mozart, who predicted a great career in music for Ludwig. By age nineteen, he was playing violin in local orchestras and giving music lessons to help support his family.

In his early twenties, Beethoven moved to Vienna, Austria, and began composing and performing as a concert pianist. Here, he took composition lessons from composer George Frideric Handel. Beethoven knew that to earn a living as a composer, he needed wealthy patrons who would help him financially. He began making friends with wealthy supporters of music. By 1795 (age twenty-five) he abandoned teaching and began composing and performing full-time.

The period 1800–1815 was prolific for Beethoven. By 1815 (age forty-five) he had completed eight symphonies, twenty-seven piano sonatas, numerous sonatas for various string instruments, ten piano trios, eleven string quartets, dozens of orchestral works, and many vocal solos and choral works.

Composing was difficult for Beethoven. He anguished over every piece. He had begun losing his hearing as a young man. By his mid-forties he gave up his performing career, devoting as much time as possible to composing. The last twelve years of his life were spent composing while he slowly but steadily became deaf.

Beethoven spent his life seeking financial support from wealthy patrons of the arts. He fell in love several times but never married; his poor origins prevented him from marrying the upper-class women he desired. In practical matters such as renting an apartment, organizing performances of his music, or publishing his music, he was a disaster.

Beethoven was short, stocky, and muscular. He dressed carelessly. He was often restless and moody, and worked at composing every morning with intense concentration. He would fly into a rage at small matters which upset him, yet he was always loyal to his friends and supporters. Those friends and supporters helped to give Beethoven the freedom to compose some of the greatest European music of the nineteenth century.

Famous Works:

His nine symphonies — for orchestra
Fidelio — an opera
Missa Solemnis — for orchestra and chorus
His twelve piano sonatas — for piano
Violin Concerto — for violin and orchestra

"Music is the electrical soil in which the spirit lives."

Ludwig van Beethoven

Hector Berlioz

Heck'-tor Bear'-lee-ohs

born December 11, 1803, La Côte-Saint-André, France
died March 8, 1869, Paris, France

A Composer of the Romantic Era

As a boy, Hector Berlioz sang in a choir at his church. He became interested in music and took lessons on guitar and piano, and read books on music theory. He wrote his first piece of music at age sixteen and sent it to a publisher, but it was rejected.

When Hector turned eighteen, his father, a doctor, sent him to Paris to study medicine. Although he was not really interested in his medical studies, Hector received a degree in science. While studying in Paris, he attended concerts and studied musical scores at the library of the Paris Conservatory of music. He also took lessons in composition, and his composition teacher encouraged him to write an opera. After receiving his degree in science, Hector enrolled at the Paris Conservatory. His father, disappointed in his son, stopped sending him any money, and Hector took a job as a choir director.

After studies at the Paris Conservatory, Berlioz became more interested in composition. In 1825 (age twenty-two) he put together a huge orchestra of 150 members. But even that didn't seem big enough. His "dream orchestra," Berlioz said, would consist of 467 instrumentalists and 360 singers. Berlioz's first famous work, *Symphonie Fantastique,* was written in 1830. He wrote it to attract a young woman he loved. The performance was a success, but his girlfriend did not attend. *Symphonie Fantastique* was one of the first examples of what is called "program music"—music that tells a story.

About this time, Berlioz won the Prix de Rome, a scholarship for creative artists and musicians to study in Rome. He had applied four times before and had been rejected each time. Winning the award meant he had to move to Rome, but Berlioz was unhappy there. He returned to Paris in 1832 (age twenty-seven) and married Henrietta Smithson, a British actress. The marriage was unsuccessful and they separated, living apart until Henrietta's death in 1853, when Berlioz remarried.

Symphonie Fantastique brought Berlioz to the attention of Niccolo Paganini, a famous violinist. Paganini commissioned Berlioz to write a virtuoso work for viola. It was completed in 1834, but Paganini did not play it until 1838. Payment for this work allowed Berlioz to write *Roméo et Juliette*, which he called a "dramatic symphony" for orchestra and chorus. He continued to compose operas and orchestral music throughout the 1830s.

In the 1840s, Berlioz toured frequently throughout Europe, often conducting his own compositions because he felt no other conductor could do justice to his music. In 1853 (age fifty-four) he became a music critic for a French magazine. He was very successful in this position and has been called the greatest music critic of his era.

Berlioz was unhappy in his later life; his second marriage turned out as bad as his first, and he suffered from health problems. He was hot-tempered, desperate for love, a braggart, and could be rude.

Famous Works:

Symphonie Fantastique — for orchestra
Le damnation de Faust — for orchestra
Roméo et Juliette — for orchestra and chorus
Te Deum — for orchestra and chorus
Requiem — for orchestra and chorus

"At least I have the modesty to admit that lack of modesty is one of my failings."
Hector Berlioz

Leonard Bernstein

His last name is pronounced Bern'-styne.

born August 25, 1918, Lawrence, Massachusetts
died October 14, 1990, New York, New York

A Composer of the Twentieth Century

As a child, Leonard Bernstein took piano lessons and frequently attended concerts in Boston with his parents. After high school, he entered Harvard University, where he majored in music and graduated with honors in 1939. Leonard then enrolled at the Curtis Institute of Music in Philadelphia, where he studied piano, conducting, and orchestration for two years.

In 1940, Bernstein attended the very first Tanglewood Music Festival, a summer music academy in Massachusetts. The Boston Symphony spent the summers at Tanglewood, and its conductor, Serge Koussevitzky, became Bernstein's mentor. He studied with Koussevitzky for four years at Tanglewood.

By the early 1940s, Bernstein had settled in New York City where he lived for the rest of his life. At the age of twenty-five, he was named assistant conductor of the New York Philharmonic. In November of 1943, he was called on, at the last minute, to substitute for the principal conductor of the Philharmonic in a particularly difficult concert. The music critics praised his performance with the orchestra and his career as a conductor took off.

Bernstein's first symphony, *Jeremiah*, was premiered in 1944. For the next decade he worked tirelessly as a conductor. As a composer during this period, he wrote a great variety of music, including orchestral works, operettas, film scores, ballets, chamber works, choral music, Broadway musicals, and songs. In 1951, he married Felicia Montealegre Cohn, a Chilean actress.

In 1957 (age thirty-nine), Bernstein wrote the music for a groundbreaking and successful musical entitled *West Side Story*. A year later, he became the first American-born conductor to be named music director of the New York Philharmonic. With the Philharmonic, he hosted a series of televised "Young People's Concerts," which ran from 1958 until 1972. He would hold the Philharmonic position until 1969 (age fifty-one). When he left, the Philharmonic honored him as "laureate conductor for life." Throughout the 1970s and 1980s, Bernstein continued composing, and maintained a busy conducting schedule around the world. He conducted his final concert, at the Tanglewood Music Festival, a few months before his death.

There have been many composers who were also fine conductors, but few excelled at both as well as Leonard Bernstein. His music spanned all genres, from popular to orchestral, and he was influenced by everything from Beethoven to jazz. Bernstein was a great music educator; his "Young People's Concerts" were some of the most successful educational television shows ever produced, and they introduced millions of young people to the joy of music. He was also an excellent pianist, but that skill was overshadowed by his other talents. Today, Leonard Bernstein is recognized as one of the America's greatest musicians, and almost certainly its greatest conductor.

Famous Works

West Side Story — a musical
Chichester Psalms — for chorus and orchestra
Jeremiah — a symphony, for orchestra
Overture to Candide — for orchestra, from an operetta
Fancy Free — a ballet

"When I am with composers, I say I am a conductor. When I am with conductors, I say I am a composer."

Leonard Bernstein

Johannes Brahms

Yo-hahn'-us Brahmz

born May 7, 1833, Hamburg, Germany
died April 3, 1897, Vienna, Austria

A Composer of the Romantic Era

Johannes Brahms, the son of an orchestral string bass player, was not a good student in school. But he excelled at the piano. He studied at first with a friend of his father, and later with the most respected music teacher in Hamburg, Germany. Johannes helped his family financially by playing popular music in dance halls.

By the age of sixteen he was performing throughout Europe as a concert pianist. During his concert tours, Brahms met many famous musicians and composers who recognized his outstanding musical talent. He became friends with another composer, Robert Schumann. At twenty-one, he took a position as conductor of a municipal orchestra in Detwold, Germany.

At Detwold, he began to devote more time to composition. In 1856 (age twenty-three), when his friend Robert Schumann died, Brahms moved to Düsseldorf, Germany to console Schumann's widow, Clara. He eventually fell in love with her. Brahms and Clara Schumann remained in love for forty years but never married. He relied on her advice and musical expertise throughout his career as a composer.

From 1859 to 1862 Brahms served as conductor of various orchestras. He finally settled in Vienna, Austria, where he lived for the rest of his life. Here he composed, conducted orchestras and choirs, and taught piano. Except for occasional tours as a concert pianist, Brahms lived a rather ordinary life in Vienna.

He began devoting more time to composing, but it wasn't until 1873 (age forty) that he had his first success, with a work for orchestra entitled *Variations on a Theme by Haydn*. He also was continuing work on a symphony which he had begun in 1854. This *First Symphony* was finally performed in 1876, twenty-two years after Brahms began composing it. He was now forty-three years old. Between 1877 and 1884 Brahms wrote three more symphonies, several concertos, and several pieces of chamber music.

For the last twenty years of his life, Brahms continued composing music in all forms except opera. He was recognized throughout Europe as a distinguished composer and honored by his adopted country, Austria. Many young composers moved to Vienna to study with him. He spent summers in the country outside of Vienna. During these summers he did much of his composing. He was very disciplined as a composer and worked hard at perfecting his craft.

In Vienna, Brahms lived a simple life, spending most of his time in a small, three room apartment. He was very sociable and had many friends, but never wanted to be the center of attention. He dressed shabbily, often in cheap, worn clothing, but he was a shrewd businessman with his music. After his death, he left an estate worth more than $100,000, most of it from royalties on his published music. That was a huge amount of money for a composer who achieved little success until the age of forty.

Famous Works:

His four symphonies — for orchestra
Requiem — for chorus and orchestra
Violin Concerto — for violin and orchestra
His songs (there were more than 200)
His choral music *Liebeslieder Waltzes* — for chorus and piano four hands

"Composing a symphony is no laughing matter!"
Johannes Brahms

Benjamin Britten

His last name rhymes with "mitten."

born November 22, 1913, Lowestoft, England
died December 4, 1976, Aldeburg, England

A Composer of the Twentieth Century

Benjamin Britten grew up in a well-to-do family; his father was a dentist and his mother an amateur singer. He took piano and viola lessons as a child, and at age thirteen began to study composition with a local teacher. After attending a boarding school, Benjamin entered the Royal College of Music in London where he focused on piano and composition. His early music showed a very mature style for such a young man; several of his student compositions were published in the 1930s. He also composed music for films, and became interested in opera.

Britten moved to the United States and lived in Amityville, New York, for a few years in the early 1940s. While in the United States he wrote several important works, including an opera, *Paul Bunyan*. He returned to England in 1942. Britten applied for, and was granted, an exemption from military service as a conscientious objector. He did, however, volunteer for service in hospitals and bomb shelters during World War II. Perhaps his most famous work, the opera *Peter Grimes,* was premiered in June, 1945, in a London theatre which was re-opening after five years of war. *Peter Grimes* was well received by audiences and music critics, and established Britten as a major international composer.

After the war, Britten founded the Aldeburgh Festival, an annual event held each June which featured performances of new operas. Eventually it grew to include other types of music, poetry, literature, drama, and art. Many of Britten's operas were first performed at Aldeburgh, often directed by Britten himself.

By the early 1950s, Britten devoted himself to composing and conducting his own music. Opera was his main interest; he composed thirteen during his lifetime. Often, however, he wrote music specifically for an individual performer. For example, he wrote several cello works for the virtuoso cellist Mstislav Rostropovich. A 1957 tour of Japan and the far East developed his interest in Eastern music, and several of his compositions after that date had Eastern influences.

Britten continued to be involved with the Aldeburgh Festival throughout his life, often presenting performances of operas which he felt had been overlooked by the public. He also composed educational music intended to be performed for children, such as *Let's Make an Opera* and *The Young Person's Guide to the Orchestra.* Many of his operas were performed on television in England.

Although Benjamin Britten is best known for his operas, he composed a great variety, and a great number, of other works. He was also a fine pianist, occasionally accompanying vocal soloists in recitals. Britten was a friend of many of the major conductors and composers of the mid-twentieth century. His music, particularly his operas, were well loved by audiences of his time, and remain popular today.

Famous Works

Billy Budd — an opera
Peter Grimes — an opera
The Turn of the Screw — an opera
War Requiem — for chorus and orchestra
The Young Person's Guide to the Orchestra — for orchestra

"If wind and water could write music, it would sound like Ben's."

Yehudi Menuhin, violinist and conductor, describing Benjamin Britten's music

Anton Bruckner

Ahn'-tone Brook'-ner

born September 4, 1824, Ansfelden, Austria
died October 11, 1896, Vienna, Austria

A Composer of the Romantic Era

As a child, Anton Bruckner took organ lessons from his father, who was a schoolteacher and organist. His father died when Anton was thirteen, and Anton was sent to a choir school to receive further musical training. He then studied to become a schoolteacher, and, after graduating, took a job as a teacher in a small village.

In 1845 (age twenty-one), Brucker returned to the choir school and joined the faculty as a music teacher and organist. For the next eight years he taught, practiced the organ for hours a day, and composed music. He left the choir school in 1853 to pursue his interest in composing. Anton moved to Vienna, an important city for music and composers. Here he studied at the Vienna Conservatory of music, and received his degree in 1861 at the age of thirty-seven.

Not until he received his degree did Bruckner feel confident to present his music to the public. His premiere was a choral work entitled *Ave Maria,* which he conducted in performance with the Vienna Choral Society. Many of his early compositions were sacred works for voices. In 1863 Bruckner heard a performance of an opera by Richard Wagner. Bruckner was greatly impressed and influenced by Wagner's music. He began to apply more contemporary and modern harmonies to his music, including his sacred music. In 1865 Brucker showed Wagner sketches for his first symphony. This time it was Wagner who was impressed, and he encouraged Bruckner to finish the work.

Bruckner joined the faculty of the Vienna Conservatory of music in 1868 (age forty-four) as a professor of organ and counterpoint. He moved into a small apartment where he lived for the rest of his life. Bruckner finished his symphony, and it was premiered with modest success. Other of his compositions did not fare as well. He was unable to get some of his works performed; musicians called them "unperformable" or "nonsense." Nevertheless, Bruckner continued composing, with greater determination than ever.

More symphonies followed (he wrote a total of nine), even though one critic suggested Bruckner throw them all in the trash. Sometimes he conducted his own music simply because no other conductor wanted to do it. Sometimes only a handful of people came to the performances. Other composers, such as Wagner and Gustav Mahler, however, praised Bruckner's music and encouraged him. So Bruckner persevered, and during the last twenty-five years of his life wrote his finest music, music that today is recognized as intelligent, complex, and important. And by the 1880s even the Viennese audiences and critics had begun to appreciate it.

Anton Bruckner was physically awkward and naive, a simple, religious, small-town man who spent his life in the big city of Vienna, and was never totally at ease there. He developed late as a composer, lacked self-confidence, and was rejected by critics and audiences until he was an old man.

Famous Works:

His nine symphonies, especially
Symphony No. 4 — for orchestra
Symphony No. 7 — for orchestra
Symphony No. 8 — for orchestra
Te Deum — for chorus and orchestra

"Bruckner! He is my man!"

Richard Wagner

Frédéric Chopin

Fred'-er-ik Shoh'-pan

born February 22 (or possibly March 1), 1810,
Zelazowa Wola, Poland
died October 17, 1849, Paris, France

A Composer of the Romantic Era

Like many other composers, Frédéric began playing piano as a child. He was extremely talented. By age eight, he was performing in concert with orchestras, and had begun to compose music for the piano. At age fifteen his *Rondo for Piano* was published and he entered the Warsaw Conservatory of music. In 1829 (age nineteen) he moved to Vienna, Austria, where he performed as a concert pianist, and where he had access to the many music publishers located there.

He returned to Warsaw a year later, where he performed the premieres of two of his piano concertos. War in Poland in 1831 forced Chopin move to France, where his father had been born, and he settled in Paris. He lived there for the rest of his life, although he stayed in touch with his native Poland through a community of Polish citizens who lived in Paris. Chopin gave his first concert in Paris in 1832, but his refined and precise style of playing was not immediately accepted by French audiences, who preferred more powerful and showy performers.

So Chopin began performing less and composing more. He also concentrated on teaching piano. He charged large fees for lessons, but always had plenty of students. He also came to realize that he was more successful as a performer when he played in small recital rooms instead of large concert halls.

Chopin's compositions for piano became extremely popular in France, with music publishers competing for the right to publish his music for piano. He became involved with the high society of Paris and fell in love with a female author named Aurore Dudevant, whose novels were published under pen name of George Sand.

In 1838–39 Chopin spent the winter on the Mediterranean island of Majorca, where he completed his twenty-five preludes for piano. However, the cold and wet weather on the island, combined with some existing health problems, nearly caused his death. But he recovered upon his return to Paris. He continued composing—primarily music for the piano—throughout the rest of the 1830s and 1840s. In fact, Chopin wrote some of his finest music, including his *Sonata in B-flat minor*, between 1838 and 1841.

By the mid 1840s, Chopin was again suffering from health problems, and his long term relationship with Aurore Dudevant was ending. In 1848 he made a brief trip to England and Scotland, and gave his last concert in Paris. He died, probably of tuberculosis, in Paris in 1849.

Although he spent most of his adult life in Paris, Frédéric Chopin is considered to be the greatest of all Polish composers. He enjoyed the company of wealthy, powerful, and famous people. He was a short, slim, sensitive, and physically frail man who, nevertheless, lived and dressed as a fashionable member of Paris society. Chopin's compositions for piano are among the greatest ever written, and he is also recognized as one of the finest pianists of his time.

Famous Works:

His twenty-five preludes for piano
His two piano concertos — for piano and orchestra
His twenty-seven etudes for piano
Sonata in B-flat minor — for piano

"Simplicity is the final achievement. After one has played a vast quantity of notes and more notes, it is simplicity that emerges as the crowning reward of art."

Frédéric Chopin

Aaron Copland

The first syllable of his last name rhymes with "hope"

born November 14, 1900, Brooklyn, New York
died December 2, 1990, New York, New York

A Composer of the Twentieth Century

Aaron Copland's family was not musical and did not encourage him to take music lessons. Nevertheless, Aaron began to study the piano at age fourteen. As a teenager he also studied music theory and began to consider composing as a career.

After high school, Aaron was accepted at a music school for American students in Paris, France, where he studied composition. His teacher was Nadia Boulanger, who later became famous because many of her students achieved great success as composers. Returning to the United States in 1924, Copland worked as a piano player at a resort hotel while composing several orchestral works. Within a year he had two compositions performed in concert and had been commissioned by the Boston Symphony to compose a work for them.

During this period, he also received a financial award from the Guggenheim Foundation, the first ever given to a musician, and won a composition contest sponsored by RCA Records. These awards allowed him to give up playing piano at the resort and spend most of his time writing music.

While in his 20s, Copland joined the League of Composers, a group whose goal was to encourage performances of new musical works. He remained active in the League of Composers throughout his life and eventually became head of its board of directors.

By the 1930s, Copland came to believe that a composer should write music for a variety of occasions and performing groups, and should not limit himself to composing just orchestral music for serious concert performance. He also began incorporating American folk and jazz melodies into his music. His most famous works were written during the 1930s and include ballets such as *Billy the Kid, Rodeo,* and *Appalachian Spring,* which won the Pulitzer Prize for music.

Copland was one of the first composers to write music for motion pictures, and during the 1930s he wrote soundtracks for several important films. He was also greatly interested in providing music for student performers, and composed several orchestral works and an opera for student groups. He also encouraged other composers to write for young performers. By the 1940s, Copland had reached his goal of composing serious, quality music for a variety of audiences without ever lowering his musical standards.

Aaron Copland was a studious man, and throughout his life he was active as a teacher and writer. He never forgot how he had to play piano at a hotel to make a living when he was a young composer. For that reason, he was active in several organizations that encouraged young composers by offering performances of their music as well as financial grants, which allowed them to spend more time composing. He was one of the first composers to take full advantage of the new technologies of the early twentieth century, including recordings, radio, and motion pictures.

Famous Works:

Billy the Kid — a ballet
Appalachian Spring — a ballet
Fanfare for the Common Man — for orchestra
Symphony No. 3 — for orchestra
The Tender Land — an opera

"So long as the human spirit thrives on this planet, music in some living form will accompany and sustain it and give it expressive meaning."

Aaron Copland

Claude Debussy

Clawd Duh-bew-see'

born August 22, 1862, Saint-Germain-en-Laye, near Paris, France
died March 25, 1918, Paris France

A Composer of the Late Romantic Era and Early Twentieth Century

When Claude Debussy was three, his father went bankrupt and sent Claude to be raised by an aunt. His aunt was a great supporter of the arts and introduced Claude to music and art by taking him to concerts and art galleries. With his aunt's support, Claude began taking piano lessons. He showed considerable talent, and at age eleven he entered the Paris Conservatory of music.

He studied off and on at the conservatory for eleven years. During those years he began composing, and several of his compositions won awards. In 1880, while still studying at the conservatory, Debussy acquired a patroness, Madame Nadezhda von Meck, the same wealthy woman who supported Russian composer Peter Tchaikovsky. Through Madame von Meck, he became familiar with Tchaikovsky's music.

When Debussy was twenty-one, one of his compositions won an award known as the Prix de Rome. As the winner, he was required to live and compose in Rome, Italy, for three years. While in Rome, he sent several compositions back to the conservatory in Paris, but they were not well received by conductors or audiences. Nor were his compositions successful with Italian audiences.

After returning to France at age twenty-five, Debussy became a part of the arts scene in Paris, which included painters, writers, poets, and composers. Here he developed a philosophy of composition in which he tried to create, musically, the same images and emotions created by the school of French painters known as Impressionists. This resulted in music much different from the music that was popular with Paris audiences of the time.

The culmination of his new philosophy was his opera *Pelléas et Mélisande*, which was performed in 1902 to mixed reviews, although audiences seemed to like it. This Impressionistic opera made Debussy famous. He now had many devoted followers, and began to compose more music for orchestra and piano in the same Impressionistic style. The music he composed between 1903 and 1910 was popular with audiences and helped to create an interest in new music for the new century.

In spite of financial and health problems for the last ten years of his life, Debussy continued working, but his final works were not as creative as his earlier ones.

Although his music was called Impressionistic, Debussy disliked the term when it was applied to his music. His music explored new harmonies which were further developed by composers who came after him. His style was a transition between the melodic music of the nineteenth century and the rhythmic music of the twentieth century.

Claude Debussy was a popular and recognized figure in early twentieth century Paris, often walking the streets in a cape and broad-brimmed hat. His greatest joy was spending time with other creative people in the many cafés of Paris.

Famous Works:

La Mer — for orchestra
Prélude à la L'Après-midi d'un faune
(Prelude to the Afternoon of a Fawn) — for orchestra
Preludes — for piano
Etudes — for piano
Nocturnes — for orchestra and female chorus

"Music is the arithmetic of sounds."

Claude Debussy

Antonín Dvořák

An'-tohn-yin Dvor'-zhok

born September 8, 1841, Nelahozeves, Bohemia (now Czechoslovakia)
died May 1, 1904, Prague, Czechoslovakia

A Composer of the Romantic Era

Antonín Dvořák's parents were innkeepers. Music was a part of his life from an early age. His father played violin in a village band and encouraged his son to take violin lessons.

At fourteen, Antonín's parents sent him to live with his uncle in Venice, Italy, where they expected Antonín to learn the innkeeping trade. Instead he spent much of his time studying the violin, viola, piano, and organ with a local teacher. At the age of sixteen, he moved to Prague, Czechoslovakia, and entered the famous Organ School of Prague. To support his studies he played in local bands and small orchestras which performed in cafés in the city.

After graduation from the organ school in 1862, Dvořák spent eleven years playing in the orchestra of the Czech National Opera. During these years he continued his studies of orchestral works and began composing.

In 1873 (age thirty-two) he became organist at a church and married Anna Cermakova. After he married, Dvořák began to take composing more seriously. His first symphony was premiered in 1874 and won an award from the Austrian government. In 1875 he wrote an opera. Dvořák now began to compose works with Bohemian folk melodies, including a set of Slavonic dances for orchestra. The *Slavonic Dances* were performed throughout Europe and became extremely popular with audiences. Suddenly Dvořák was famous and his works were in great demand.

In 1884, he traveled to London to conduct his works with orchestras there. The trip was a success and several of his works were published by a British publisher. Now financially successful, he purchased a country villa in which to spend his summers.

In 1892 (age fifty-one), Dvořák was invited to become director of the National Conservatory of Music in New York City at the huge salary (in 1892) of $15,000 per year. He agreed and moved to New York. During the summers, when the conservatory closed, he spent his time at an arts community in Iowa. Here he wrote a symphony entitled *From the New World*, which incorporated several African-American melodies. He also wrote several works based on the music of Native Americans.

Homesick for his native country, Dvořák left his position with the National Conservatory in 1895 and returned to Prague. Upon his return, he composed his most famous work for piano, *Humoresque*. Eventually, he was appointed director of the Prague Conservatory, a position which he held for the rest of his life.

Antonín Dvořák was a highly regarded composer, both in Europe and the United States. He was a simple man with few artistic or creative interests beyond music. He enjoyed his summer home in the country and his family. He was not a gifted composer and writing did not come easy to him. Rather, Dvořák was a hard worker, who slowly but methodically created some of the finest orchestral music of the late nineteenth century.

Famous Works:

From the New World — a symphony for orchestra
Slavonic Dances — for orchestra
Requiem — for chorus and orchestra
Serenade — for string orchestra
Songs My Mother Taught Me — for voice and piano

"All the great musicians have borrowed from the songs of the common people."
Antonín Dvořák

Edward Elgar

His name is pronounced as it is spelled

born June 2, 1857, Broadheath (near Worcester), England
died February 23, 1934, Worcester, England

A Composer of the Late Romantic Era and Early Twentieth Century

Edward Elgar's early life revolved around music; his father ran a music store, played violin, and served as a church organist. Edward studied violin and piano with local music teachers. His father wanted Edward to become a lawyer, so at sixteen Edward moved to London, England, to study law. But he soon returned home to play in local orchestras. He also gave organ and violin recitals and composed music for local groups.

Until the age of thirty-two, Edward had no focus in life. He wasn't talented enough to become a successful concert performer and was content to perform at local concerts, compose for local groups, and work at various jobs. He was appreciated in his home town but had no wider fame, either as a composer or as a performer. At thirty-two he married, and his wife, Alice, convinced him that he should take composing more seriously. They moved to London and Alice became Edward's greatest supporter.

In London, he began writing serious concert music. However, neither he nor Alice enjoyed life in London, so they moved to the country town of Malvern. Here Elgar began composing choral music. To earn an income, he taught organ and violin. During the 1890s, he received a few commissions which earned him some income.

Elgar's first success was an orchestral work written in 1899 (age forty-three) entitled *Enigma Variations*. This composition became one of the most popular and successful orchestral works by a British composer. Other successes followed, including an oratorio, *The Dream of Gerontius*. In 1900 the British government commissioned him to write music for the coronation of King Edward VII. This music was much loved by the British people.

Elgar's most successful period as a composer was 1900-1914. His *First Symphony*, written in 1908, was performed over 100 times throughout Europe in its first year. From 1905 to 1913 he was a professor of music at Birmingham University in England, and during World War I he wrote military music for the British government. By 1920 he had produced two symphonies, a violin concerto, numerous overtures, oratorios, chamber music, and choral works.

When his wife died in 1920, Elgar stopped composing, but he continued to conduct performances of his music. In 1934 he wrote one final piece, a hymn for King George V, who had been ill.

Edward Elgar was a friendly, practical, and personable man. He was devoted to his wife, Alice, who supported and encouraged him. Elgar was an excellent teacher and probably would have spent his life as a music professor were it not for Alice's encouragement of his career as a composer. He was very patriotic and supported England by composing music for state occasions. He was one of the first composers to realize the value of recordings (then known as gramophone recordings) and made recordings of his music as early as 1914.

Famous Works:

Pomp and Circumstance — from *Six Military Marches for Orchestra*
Symphony No. 1 — for orchestra
The Dream of Gerontius — an oratorio for two choirs, soloists, and orchestra
Enigma Variations — for orchestra
Concerto for Violin and Orchestra

"Music is in the air; you simply take as much of it as you want."

Edward Elgar

Duke Ellington

(real name: Edward Kennedy Ellington)

His name is pronounced as it is spelled

born April 29, 1899, Washington, DC
died May 24, 1974, New York, New York

A Composer of the Twentieth Century

Edward Kennedy Ellington was given the nickname Duke when he was a child. He was known by that name for the rest of his life. Duke grew up in Washington, DC, and his parents encouraged his interest art, music, and sports. Duke took piano lessons as a boy, and as a teenager he began to write songs and improvise at the keyboard. After high school, Duke received a scholarship to study art at Pratt Institute in Brooklyn, New York. Duke, however, was more interested in music, so he stayed in Washington and picked up jobs as a pianist with various jazz bands. At age nineteen he married Edna Thompson.

In 1923, Duke formed his own band and took it to New York City. During the next few years, he began to compose music for the band, which had grown in size to become what is known as a jazz "big band." Ellington played piano in the band. He was known as a strong leader, and he hired only the best musicians. For the rest of his his life, Ellington led his big band, using it as his "instrument" for his compositions, of both jazz and concert music.

Ellington embraced the new technologies, such as recordings and radio, which developed during the 1920s. His first recording was released in 1927. Duke entered into an agreement with a major music publisher to print sheet music of his jazz songs. They sold extremely well, as did popular recordings by his band. He composed his first film score in 1929 (age thirty), just a few years after sound was added to motion pictures.

The Ellington band worked steadily through the 1930s, playing popular night clubs such as the Cotton Club, in Harlem, New York. By 1940 (age forty-one), however, Duke had turned his attention to serious composing for instrumental ensembles. Sales of sheet music and recordings remained his main sources of income. This gave him the freedom to compose music which was more serious in nature—music for the concert hall. In the 1940s, the band began to play concert venues such as Carnegie Hall, in New York City, performing orchestral suites composed by Ellington.

The jazz/big band era declined after World War II, but Ellington kept his band on the road. A performance at the Newport (Rhode Island) Jazz Festival in 1956 rejuvenated his career and added new, younger fans. In the 1960s Ellington and his longtime arranger, Billy Strayhorn, transcribed music by composers such as Peter Tchaikovsky and Edvard Grieg for the Ellington band.

Duke Ellington pushed jazz and American music into new musical territory. Like composer George Gershwin (they were born seven months apart), Ellington began in the jazz world and moved into the concert world. He composed thousands of songs and short jazz works for his band as well as large orchestral works. He has frequently been described as a national musical treasure, and he was the recipient of dozens of awards. One was the Presidential Medal of Freedom, the highest civilian award given by the United States.

Famous Works:

Black, Brown and Beige — a suite for orchestra
Anatomy of a Murder — motion picture score
The Far East Suite — for jazz band
His popular songs
His music for jazz band

"A problem is a chance to do your best."

Duke Ellington

César Franck

Ses'-air Frahnk

born December 10, 1822. Liège, Belgium
died November 8, 1890, Paris, France

A Composer of the Romantic Era

César Franck's father was a banker who loved music. He paid for piano lessons for his son, and by age eleven, César made a concert tour of Belgium. Two years later he won first prize for piano playing at the Liège Conservatory of music. All his teachers agreed that César should study in Paris, home of the greatest pianists of the time. So the Franck family moved to Paris and César enrolled at the Paris Conservatory of music. Here he continued to win prizes and awards for his piano playing.

By age fifteen César began composing and completed a piano concerto. His father was distressed that César seemed more interested in composing than in performing. He withdrew César from the Paris Conservatory, moved the family back to Belgium, and arranged a concert tour for his son. César returned to Paris in 1844, now totally dedicated to composition. He also renewed his religious faith, and he began to compose sacred music. He married in 1848.

For the next several years, Franck did little performing as a concert pianist. He composed, but his music was rarely performed. He became a more private person, focused on his religion. When he was thirty, Franck switched from piano to organ. He played organ in a classical style, similar to the way Bach had played more than a century earlier. In 1858 (age thirty-six) he became organist at a large Catholic church in Paris.

For the next several years Franck's life settled into a routine. He would rise early in the morning and compose for several hours before spending the rest of the day teaching voice, piano, and organ at a private school. Some of his music was performed but with little success. Franck devoted considerable time and energy to an opera, but was unable to get it produced. This caused him great stress and, at one point, he nearly had a nervous breakdown.

In 1866 the composer Franz Liszt heard Franck play the organ and pronounced Franck the finest organist since Bach. Franck returned to the Paris Conservatory as an organ instructor in 1872 (age fifty). He also took on some composition students. His mind was always on his own composing, however; sometimes he would simply walk out of a lesson in order to work on his music. His students, however, accepted his odd habits and were greatly influenced by his music.

By the 1880s, Franck was composing the best music of his life. A concert of his music was presented by his students in Paris a few years before his death. Many of the compositions were not well performed but Franck was pleased to hear his music brought to life.

César Franck developed late as a composer. Much of his music was rarely performed, or performed poorly, during his lifetime. He lacked the drive and determination to get his music played by fine orchestras. And some of his early music was simply not very good. But by the end of his life, Franck had produced an outstanding body of work, and many of his later compositions are still performed today.

Famous Works:

Symphony in D minor — for orchestra
Sonata for Piano and Violin
Le Chasseur Maudit — for orchestra
The Beatitudes — an oratorio for chorus and orchestra
Three Chorales — for organ

"I fancy he is lacking in that convenient social sense that opens all doors."

Franz Liszt, describing César Franck

George Gershwin

His last name is pronounced Gur'-shwin

born September 26, 1898, New York, New York
died July 11, 1937, Los Angeles, California

A Composer of the Twentieth Century

George Gershwin's parents were born in Russia, moved to the United States, and settled in New York City. The family moved frequently when George was a child; George and his brother Ira once counted twenty-five apartments in which the family lived. When George was about twelve, his mother bought a second-hand piano. To everyone's surprise, George immediately sat down and played several popular songs. In fact, George had been practicing the piano at a friend's house.

Eventually, George took piano lessons and learned to read music. He quit high school at fifteen, and took a job as a pianist for a popular music publisher. By the time he was nineteen, George was writing his own popular songs, with lyrics by others, including his brother Ira. Little by little, George's popular songs began to achieve some success. By 1919, he was writing songs for Broadway musicals.

Beginning in 1924 (age twenty-six), George and his brother Ira wrote a string of very successful Broadway musicals including *Oh, Kay!*, *Strike Up the Band*, and *Of Thee I Sing*, which, in 1932, became the first musical to win a Pulitzer Prize for Drama. In addition to his Broadway shows, Gershwin also composed music for the concert stage. His first concert work, *Rhapsody in Blue*, was originally written for jazz band and piano, but was later scored for orchestra and piano. It was premiered in 1924, with great success, in a concert promoted as "An Experiment in Modern Music." *Rhapsody in Blue* is often cited as the first serious concert work which incorporated jazz.

Several more successful concert works followed, including *Piano Concerto in F*, and an orchestral work, *An American in Paris*. Throughout the 1920s, Gershwin traveled to Europe five times, to work and study with famous composers. While in Paris, he studied with the legendary composition teacher Nadia Boulanger. He also studied composition and counterpoint with American composers Henry Cowell and Wallingford Riegger.

Gershwin's most famous concert work was the opera *Porgy and Bess*, which was based on a novel set in Charleston, South Carolina. It premiered in Boston in September, 1935, played New York for sixteen weeks, then toured the country for three months. *Porgy and Bess* is one of the first operas to have an all black cast, and is considered one of the most important American operas of the twentieth century. Gershwin also toured as a pianist and conductor, performing and presenting his own music to audiences as large as 18,000. He moved to California in 1936 to work on film scores for Hollywood. Gershwin was working on his third score when he died of a brain tumor in Los Angeles at the age of thirty-eight.

George Gershwin is considered one of the true geniuses of American music. No other composer was so successful in the worlds of both concert and popular music. His concert music was praised by audiences, critics, and other serious composers. And his popular songs, mostly from his Broadway shows of the 1920s, remain extremely popular with singers and jazz artists.

Famous Works:

Rhapsody in Blue — for orchestra and piano
Concerto in F — for orchestra and piano
An American in Paris — for orchestra
Porgy and Bess — an opera
Preludes for Piano

"True music must repeat the thought and inspirations of the people and the time. My people are Americans and my time is today."

George Gershwin

Christoph Gluck

Kris'-toff Glook

born July 2, 1714, Erasbach (Bavaria), Germany
died November 15, 1787, Vienna, Austria

A Composer of the Classical Era

Christoph Gluck attended village schools in the rural Bavarian region of Germany, where his father was a forester. In school, he learned to play string instruments and took voice lessons. After completing his public schooling, Christoph moved to Prague, Czechoslovakia, where he was able to support himself by singing and playing violin in churches. In 1736 (age twenty-two), he moved to Vienna, Austria, where he was befriended and supported by various princes and noblemen. He accompanied one of them, Prince Melzi, on a trip to Milan, Italy.

In Milan, Gluck became greatly interested in composition, Italian church music, and, most importantly, opera. For the next four years, he took composition lessons from several Italian teachers. In 1741, Gluck completed his first opera, *Artaserse,* which was presented in Milan to great success. He promptly wrote seven more operas in the next three years. Gluck visited Paris and London in 1745 (age thirty-one). In London, he was commissioned by an Italian opera company to write two operas, which he completed in less than a year.

In 1746, Gluck took a position as conductor for a traveling Italian opera company, and in 1750 he married Marianna Pergin, daughter of a wealthy businessman. They settled in Vienna, where Gluck met and befriended a poet, Ranieri de Calzabigi. Together, Gluck and Calzabigi set out to reform opera. The two developed a belief that music should enhance an opera's libretto (its story) by adding dramatic effect. Also, the pair agreed with audiences who wanted operas based on more real-life, modern situations, as opposed to fables and stories of ancient times.

Calzabigi began writing modern opera librettos which Gluck set to music. Several were great successes, including *Orfeo ed Euridice* (1762), and *Alceste* (1767) and *Paride ed Elena* (1770). The Gluck/Calzabigi operas produced in Milan in the 1760s significantly changed the direction of opera, and greatly influenced the next major opera composer, Wolfgang Amadeus Mozart.

In 1773 (age fifty-nine), Gluck moved to Paris. In Paris, there was great disagreement about who was the better opera composer, Gluck or Niccolo Piccinni, an Italian composer. Gluck's masterpiece, *Iphigénie en Tauride,* written in 1779, left no doubt that Gluck was superior to any other opera composer of his time. (Piccinni's opera on the same subject was premiered in 1781, with less success.)

After completing *Iphigénie en Tauride,* Gluck's health began to fail and he returned to Vienna, where he lived for the rest of his life. He is one of the great names in the world of opera, and had tremendous influence on its development. He composed about fifty operas and, except for a few ballets, wrote little else. Gluck frequently prepared and rehearsed the singers and orchestra for his operas. He had little patience with his singers, often rehearsing them for long hours, and accusing them of "screaming" rather than singing.

Famous Works:

Don Juan — a ballet
Orfeo ed Euridice — an opera
Alceste — an opera
Paride ed Elena — an opera
Iphigénie en Tauride — an opera

"I sought to reduce music to its true function, that of seconding poetry in order to strengthen the emotional expression."
Christoph Gluck

Edvard Grieg

Ed'-vard Greeg

born June 15, 1843, Bergen, Norway
died September 4, 1907, Bergen, Norway

A composer of the Romantic Era

Edvard Grieg's mother was an amateur pianist, and Edvard took piano lessons from her when he was a child. He studied the traditional keyboard music of composers such as Mozart and Bach. When Edvard was fifteen, he entered the Leipzig (Germany) Conservatory of music, where he studied piano and music theory. At the conservatory, he was very much influenced by the music of the German composers of the early Romantic era, such as Felix Mendelssohn.

In 1863 (age twenty), he moved to Copenhagen, Denmark. Here Grieg met his future wife, Nina Hagerup. Nina was a singer, and Grieg composed many songs for her to perform in recitals. He also began to compose music for piano. In 1867, Greg married Nina, moved to Norway, and founded the Norwegian Academy of Music. Grieg taught at the school and conducted the orchestra. He discovered, in 1868, a collection of Norwegian folk songs which greatly interested him. Folk melodies became the basis for many of Grieg's compositions, including his *Piano Concerto in A minor,* which he wrote at the age of twenty-five.

Grieg traveled to Italy in 1869 where he met the composer and pianist Franz Liszt. Liszt played the *Piano Concerto in A minor* and pronounced it a masterpiece. He encouraged Grieg to devote more time to composing. When Grieg returned to Norway, he was determined to become a successful composer. His compositions of the early 1870s became very popular with Norwegian audiences. The government of Norway recognized his work by giving him an annual salary. This enabled him to devote full time to composing.

In 1876 (age thirty-three), Grieg met Norwegian playwright Henrik Ibsen. Nine years earlier, Ibsen had written a "play in verse," entitled *Peer Gynt,* which was intended to be read rather than performed. Ibsen planned to present a stage production of the play and asked Grieg to write incidental music for the production. Both the play and the music were a great success. Grieg combined the music into a suite for orchestra, and it has become his most popular work.

After his success with *Peer Gynt,* Grieg toured throughout Europe as a pianist and conductor. He also spent time in the mountains of Norway, first at his cabin in the Hardanger region of the country and later in the town of Troldhaugen. Here he continued to compose and collect folk songs throughout the 1880s and 1890s.

Edvard Grieg is considered a nationalistic composer because his music was representative of his native country. He was much loved by Norwegians and he is considered Norway's greatest composer. His music, like that of Béla Bartók, was influenced by folk songs. His compositions are, for the most part, smaller works. Grieg wrote no operas, and although he wrote works for orchestra, he composed no symphonies. His music was traditional in style.

Famous Works:

Peer Gynt — a suite for orchestra
Piano Concerto in A minor — for orchestra and piano
His songs (there are more than 120)
Four Norwegian Dances — for orchestra
Wedding Day at Troldhaugen — for piano

"I am sure my music has a taste of codfish in it."
Edvard Grieg

George Frideric Handel

Jorj Frid'-ur-ic Hahn'-dl

born February 23, 1685, Halle (Saxony), Germany
died April 14, 1759, London, England

A Composer of the Baroque Era

As a child, George Frideric Handel showed a great deal of musical talent and planned to pursue music as a career. His local music teachers taught him as much as they could and encouraged his parents to further George's musical studies. His father, however, wanted George to become a lawyer. At the age of seventeen, George entered the University of Halle, in Germany, to study law. He maintained his interest in music by playing the organ at a nearby cathedral.

When his father died during George's first year at the university, George left school and joined an opera orchestra in Hamburg, Germany, as a violinist. Here he began composing his first opera.

At twenty-two, he moved to Italy to study opera. Italian audiences enjoyed opera, and Italy had dozens of excellent opera companies. Europe's finest opera singers and composers all spent time in Italy, hoping to achieve success with Italian audiences. Most of Handel's early operas and oratorios had Italian texts and were first performed in Italy.

In 1710 (age twenty-five), he returned to Germany but soon left for England. Here he continued to write operas and sacred choral music, now with English instead of Italian texts. After a brief return to Germany in 1712, he moved back to England, where he lived for the rest of his life. He became a British citizen in 1726.

In 1720 (age thirty-five), Handel was named artistic director of a new opera company, the Royal Academy of Music. During the next seven years, he wrote fourteen operas for the academy, as well as several oratorios. He also conducted the performances of his own operas. When the Royal Academy went bankrupt in 1728, he formed his own opera company for which he wrote thirteen more operas. In 1737, this opera company also failed. Financially, Handel lost everything and suffered a stroke. It was the lowest point of his life, and he never totally regained his health.

Now, at the age of fifty-three, Handel virtually gave up writing operas and turned his attention to oratorios. His oratorios, all in English, were hugely successful and popular in England and Ireland. He wrote his most famous oratorio, *Messiah*, in 1742, and it was an immediate success.

Handel was blunt and outspoken, and as a conductor, he could be very difficult and stubborn. But he was an honorable and respected composer, and except for the failure of his opera company he handled his finances well. He took his work seriously and wrote rapidly; in fact, he composed almost as fast as he (or a copyist) could copy the notes.

George Handel wrote his first vocal music in German, his first operas in Italian, and his most famous oratorios in English. No other composer of vocal music has successfully written vocal music in so many languages.

Famous Works:

Messiah — an oratorio for chorus and orchestra
Music for Royal Fireworks — for orchestra
Water Music — for orchestra
His forty-five operas
His sacred choral works

"I am sorry if I have only succeeded in entertaining them; I wished to make them better."

George Frideric Handel, after the first performance of *Messiah.*

Franz Joseph Haydn

Frahntz Yoh'-zef Hide'-n

born March 31, 1732, Rohrau, Austria
died May 31, 1809, Vienna, Austria

A Composer of the Classical Era

Franz Joseph Haydn was the second of twelve children. His family was quite poor. When Franz was six, his parents sent him to live with a family relative, Johann Frankh, in Hainburg, Austria. Mr. Frankh was a private music teacher and gave Franz lessons on the harpsichord, violin, and in music harmony and theory. In Hainburg, young Franz sang in a church boychoir and eventually became the chief soloist for the group.

When Franz turned seventeen and became too old for the boychoir, he made a living playing harpsichord and violin. He also began composing and completed his first mass at age nineteen, his first string quartet at twenty-three, and his first symphony at twenty-seven.

He married his wife, Anna, in 1760. They separated a few years later but Haydn continued to support Anna for the rest of her life.

In 1761 (age twenty-nine), he became the assistant choirmaster to Prince Paul Esterhazy, an Austrian prince who was a great admirer of music. Haydn eventually became a full-time court musician and lived and worked in the Esterhazy palace for twenty-nine years, until the prince's death in 1790. His daily routine required him to provide music for family concerts, private performances, and worship services. The prince also had an excellent orchestra which regularly performed Haydn's compositions.

Living in the palace, Haydn was cut off from the musical centers of Europe and, except for a few brief trips to Vienna, Austria, was not exposed to the music of other composers. He therefore developed his own style of music. He was not influenced by other composers with the exception of Wolfgang Amadeus Mozart, who Haydn met in 1781. When they met, Haydn was forty-nine and Mozart was twenty-five. Nevertheless, the older Haydn was influenced by the younger Mozart.

In 1791, after the death of Prince Esterhazy, Haydn traveled to London where he was highly regarded by British royalty. Here he heard the music of George Frideric Handel and was much impressed with Handel's oratorios. In 1795 he returned permanently to Austria and settled in Vienna where he wrote the *Emperor's Hymn*, which is now the national anthem of Austria. Inspired by Handel, Haydn also wrote several successful oratorios. By his mid-60s, Haydn's health was failing. For the last ten years of his life he wrote little, although he frequently attended concert performances of his music.

Franz Joseph Haydn was a personable man, generous and honorable. He was greatly respected by royalty throughout Europe. He wrote a large number of works and was very industrious as a composer. He was fortunate to have a patron, Prince Esterhazy, who gave him the freedom to write music for a variety of occasions. However, it was not until Haydn was over forty that his music was successful in concert halls outside the Esterhazy palace.

Famous Works:

Symphony in G Major (Surprise Symphony) — for orchestra
The Creation — an oratorio for chorus and orchestra
Mass in Time of War — an oratorio for chorus and orchestra
His fifteen operas (five others have been lost)
His fifty-two sonatas for piano

"Melody is the main thing; harmony is useful only to charm the ear."

Franz Joseph Haydn

Fanny Mendelssohn Hensel

Fan'-ny Mehn'-del-sohn Hehn'-sul

born November, 14, 1805, Hamburg, Germany
died May 14, 1847, Berlin, Germany

A Composer of the Romantic Era

Fanny Mendelssohn Hensel was the older sister, by four years, of composer Felix Mendelssohn. The Mendelssohn family was wealthy, well-educated, and active in cultural affairs. Fanny and Felix were born in Hamburg, Germany. In 1811, the Mendelssohn family moved to Berlin, Germany, because of a threat of war. Fanny first studied piano with her mother, and later studied with respected teachers in Berlin.

In 1813, the family briefly lived in Paris, France. Here Fanny continued her piano studies and her education. By age thirteen, she was a very talented pianist. As part of Fanny's education, her parents encouraged her to attend lectures and studies in physics. She wrote her first song, in honor of her father's birthday, in 1819, at the age of fourteen. But it wasn't until 1827 (age twenty-two) that two of her songs were published. Later, several of her songs were published with her brother Felix listed as the composer. Composing was not yet considered respectable for a young lady.

In 1822, when Fanny was seventeen, the Mendelssohn family began a tradition of Sunday afternoon concerts in their home, sometimes featuring music written by Fanny or Felix. Family friends, poets, writers, and other creative people were invited as guests. Fanny continued the Sunday afternoon concert tradition for the rest of her life, taking over the role of hostess after her mother's death in 1842. Although she was an excellent pianist, Fanny rarely performed in public concerts, and limited her performances to the Mendelssohn Sunday concerts.

Fanny married Wilhelm Hensel, a painter, in 1829 (age twenty-four). Together they traveled throughout Europe, and eventually spent several years in Italy.

During the first half of the nineteenth century, women were not encouraged to write music; they were not believed to have the proper artistic talent. Indeed, both Fanny's father and her brother, Felix, discouraged her from writing music. But Fanny's husband and mother persuaded her to continue. Eventually her husband suggested she submit some of her compositions to a music publisher. She did, and several of her songs were published—this time under her own name.

Like other female composers of her era, Fanny composed mostly piano music and songs—music designed to be performed at small, private gatherings, as opposed to the concert hall. In all, she composed more than 400 pieces of music.

Throughout her life, Fanny was a great supporter of her brother Felix's music, and Felix relied upon her musical advice. Although she wrote several oratorios and cantatas, as well as small instrumental works such as trios and quartets, Fanny Mendelssohn Hensel is best known for her songs and piano compositions. She died of a stroke at the age of forty-one while rehearsing one of Felix's compositions for a family Sunday concert.

Famous Works:
Her songs
Her piano music
Piano Trio in D minor — for piano, violin, and cello

"A musician beyond comparison, a remarkable pianist, and a woman of superior mind."

Composer Charles Gounod,
describing Fanny Mendelssohn Hensel

Hildegard von Bingen

Hill'-duh-gahrd fun Bing'-en
("von Bingen" refers to the town where Hildegard lived. "Von" means "from" in German, and Bingen is a town. She is referred to as Hildegard, not "von Bingen.")

born in 1098, Bemersheim, Germany
died in 1179 (probably September 17), Rupertsberg, near Bingen, Germany

A Composer of the Medieval Era

Even though Hildegard von Bingen lived approximately 900 years ago, we know quite a bit about her. Throughout her life she kept journals and exchanged many letters with others. Her father was a nobleman, her mother a noblewoman. Hildegard was their tenth child, and tradition required that the tenth child should be dedicated to the church. When Hildegard was eight, her parents sent her to a convent which was part of a monastery. Here she joined a religious order led by a nun known as Jutta of Spanheim, who many believed was a psychic and mystic. Hildegard became a nun at fifteen.

When Jutta died in 1136, Hildegard succeeded her as the Mother Superior of the order. She was thirty-eight. Within a few years, she claimed to have visions from God, and, eventually, she began writing down those visions. The church considered her a prophetess and visionary, and many church members began to seek her advice on personal and religious matters.

Sometime between 1147 and 1150 Hildegard founded a new monastery near Rudesheim, Germany. She wrote at great length on many subjects, and she exchanged letters with popes, kings, dukes, archbishops, and politicians. Many important and powerful men consulted her on matters of church and state. She also wrote poems and set at least seventy-seven of them to music.

During Hildegard's time, music for the church consisted of chants which were sung by male monks. Hildegard, however, composed her music to be sung by the nuns of her order. No other composer of the period wrote music for female voices.

Hildegard seemed to write endlessly, both music and text. She wrote an encyclopedia describing various herbal medicines she had developed. This caused people to visit her to ask her to prescribe various herbs for their illnesses. She wrote biographies of several saints, numerous religious books, and even a play. She composed much of her music between 1150 and 1160.

At age sixty, Hildegard began traveling and preaching throughout Germany. She was controversial during her lifetime. She claimed to have mystical powers, but not everyone believed her. In 1165 she moved her order of nuns to Bingen, Germany. After her death at age eighty-one, there were several efforts to canonize her, but all the efforts failed.

Hildegard was not educated in the true sense of the word. All her knowledge came from her religious training. Her music is known as plainsong chant, the type of music sung in churches during the Middle Ages. But Hildegard's compositions are unique because they were written for female voices. She often claimed that she received her music and her writings directly from God. Because of her many writings, Hildegard is considered one of the greatest women of the Middle Ages.

Famous Works:
Ordo Virtutum (Play of the Virtues) — for voices
Kyrie Eleison — for voices
Symphonia armoniae celestium revelationum — for voices

"There is Music of Heaven in all things, and we have forgotten how to hear it until we sing."
Hildegard von Bingen

Charles Ives

His last name rhymes with "wives"

born October 20, 1874, Danbury, Connecticut
died May 19, 1954, New York, New York

A Composer of the Twentieth Century

Charles Ives's father was a bandleader during the American Civil War and continued directing bands and teaching music after the war. Charles had much musical talent and took music lessons from his father. He became a church organist by the age of thirteen and, while in his teens, began to compose music. As an experiment, he sometimes composed in two keys at the same time. For example, he would write the right hand of a piano piece in one key and the left hand in another.

At twenty, Charles entered college at Yale where he studied music. While at Yale, he composed two traditional symphonies, but after graduation he decided against a career in music. Instead, he became an insurance agent in New York City. In 1907 (age thirty-three), he co-founded the Ives & Myrick Insurance Agency, and within twenty years it was the largest insurance agency in the United States. However, Charles did not abandon music, and during this period he composed steadily.

He wrote at night, on weekends, even on vacation. He tried to get choral directors and conductors interested in his music, but they would take one look at the manuscript and say the music was unperformable. In fact, it was unlike any music most musicians had ever seen. When friends suggested he write differently, or in a more traditional style, Ives would reply that he just couldn't do it.

Eventually he gave up trying to get his music performed in concerts. With his own money, he began to hire musicians to play some of his compositions.

In 1918 (age forty-four), Ives suffered a heart attack. His dual life of running a successful insurance agency and composing music had taken its toll on his health. Although he lived forty more years, he composed very little music during the rest of his life. He also began working less in the insurance agency, and in 1930 (age fifty-six), he retired from the business.

Because he could not interest any music publishers in publishing his music, Ives published, with his own money, a collection of 114 songs which he had written. He gave copies away to libraries, singers, and anyone who might want a copy. He also published other of his works including his *Concord Sonata* for piano.

By the mid 1930s, some younger composers and performers began to discover Ives's music. In 1939, twenty-one years after Ives stopped composing, a concert pianist performed his *Concord Sonata* at a recital in New York City. It was the first successful public performance of a work by Charles Ives. He was sixty-five.

Finally, in 1947 his third symphony, *The Camp Meeting*, was performed and won a Pulitzer Prize. The work had been composed thirty-six years earlier. In 1951, the New York Philharmonic premiered his Second Symphony, fifty years after it was written. Ives listened to the performance on the radio. His fourth symphony was not performed until 1965, nine years after his death.

Famous Works:

Concord Sonata — for piano, flute, and viola
Symphony No. 3 (The Camp Meeting) — for orchestra
114 Songs — for voice and piano
Variations on "America" — for orchestra
The Circus Band — for bass soloist, chorus, and orchestra

"The impossibilities of today are the possibilities of tomorrow."

Charles Ives, after someone told him his music was impossible to perform.

Scott Joplin

His name is pronounced as it is spelled

born between June, 1867 and January 1868 (exact date unknown), in west Texas (exact location unknown)
died April 1, 1917, New York, New York

A Composer of the Late Romantic Era and Early Twentieth Century

Scott Joplin's parents were musical, and after the family moved to Texarkana, Texas, Scott took piano lessons as a child. He eventually became an fine pianist. In 1893, at the age of twenty-five, he moved to Chicago where he organized a band to perform at the Columbian Exposition, a world's fair. Here he began writing down some of the piano music which he had composed but had previously performed only from memory.

After the Columbia Exposition, Joplin moved to Sedalia, Missouri, to study music at George R. Smith College, a school for African-Americans. Some of his early compositions were published, but he had his first success at age thirty-one with a piano piece entitled *Maple Leaf Rag*. *Maple Leaf Rag* was published by a St. Louis publisher and sold over one million copies, a huge success, which earned Joplin a great deal of money. With this sudden fame as a composer, he married and moved to St. Louis to become the pianist and musical director of an opera company owned by his music publisher.

Joplin continued writing ragtime piano music, a style with a syncopated (rhythmically uneven) right-hand melody line over a steady bass and harmony in the left hand. Between 1900 and 1906 he wrote more than fifty piano rags, including his most famous, *The Entertainer*.

After 1906 (age thirty-eight), Joplin began to compose larger, more extended works, including a ballet, *The Ragtime Dance*, and an opera, *A Guest of Honor*, the score of which, unfortunately, has been lost. Both were performed in St. Louis.

In 1907 (age forty), Joplin divorced his wife, moved to New York City, and began work on a major opera, *Treemonisha*, which he completed in 1911. Joplin wrote both the libretto (the words which the opera singers sing) and the music for *Treemonisha*. Rarely do composers write both the libretto and music for an opera. When his publisher would not publish this work, Joplin published it himself. He made several attempts to have *Treemonisha* performed but failed to interest any producers in the opera, and he was unable to afford a production himself.

Discouraged by his unsuccessful attempts to produce *Treemonisha*, Joplin remarried and spent the rest of his life in New York composing and teaching. In 1915, he finally put together a poorly performed version of *Treemonisha*, without scenery. Not until 1972, fifty-five years after his death, was *Treemonisha* given a full performance. In addition to the piano rags, the ballet, and the opera, Joplin also composed marches and waltzes.

Just as Wolfgang Amadeus Mozart and Johannes Brahms composed piano music based on popular dances of the time (such as minuets and waltzes), Scott Joplin composed piano pieces in a form popular in early twentieth century America: ragtime. His music was enjoyed by millions of amateur musicians, who performed his music on the piano. They also listened to his music on a new invention: the player piano, a device which allowed music to be performed mechanically on a piano.

Famous Works:

Maple Leaf Rag — for piano
The Entertainer — for piano
Magnetic Rag — for piano
His dozens of other ragtime pieces for piano
Treemonisha — an opera

"It is never right to play ragtime fast."

Scott Joplin

Franz Liszt

Frahnts List

born October 22, 1811, Raiding, Hungary
died July 30, 1886, Bayreuth, Germany

A Composer of the Romantic Era

Franz Liszt's father was an amateur musician who encouraged his son's interest in music. By age nine, Franz was an accomplished pianist. His parents took him to Vienna, Austria, in 1822 to meet the famous composer Ludwig van Beethoven. When Beethoven heard Franz perform, he was so impressed that he rushed on stage and kissed the young boy on his forehead. At least that's the story that Franz's father told for the rest of his life.

In addition to Beethoven, the young Franz also impressed the audiences and music critics of Vienna. He began taking lessons in composition from several respected teachers, and eventually moved to Paris where he hoped to study at the Paris Conservatory of music. Although he was not accepted at the conservatory, Franz remained in Paris, where, still in his teens, he performed as a concert pianist.

As a young pianist in Paris, Franz was influenced by the many great virtuoso violinists who lived and performed there. He set out to develop a performing style on the piano that was equally demanding. To accommodate his need for showy and flamboyant music in his concerts, Liszt began writing his own music to perform. He used the term "recital" for his concerts, a word that had not been previously used for a performance, but is now commonly used.

Liszt continued as a concert pianist throughout Europe until 1847 (age thirty-six). His concert tour of Russia in 1842 established his reputation as the finest pianist in Europe—which almost certainly meant the finest pianist in the world. In 1848, Liszt retired from concert performing and began concentrating totally on composition, including orchestral music. He moved to Weimar, Germany, and became the official composer of the court of Weimar. In this position, Liszt helped to develop Weimar as an important city for music. He conducted many new works by the composers Richard Wagner and Hector Berlioz, including several world premieres.

In 1860 (age forty-nine), Liszt moved to Rome where he began writing sacred music. By 1869 he was dividing his time between Rome, Vienna, and Budapest, Hungary. In the final years of his life, Liszt devoted himself to teaching composition, and he took on many composition students. He did a final concert tour of Paris and London to celebrate his seventy-fifth birthday in 1886.

Franz Liszt was a handsome man, popular with women throughout his life. He was a brilliant, thoughtful musician and is recognized as one of the greatest pianists in history. He greatly advanced performance techniques for the piano. Liszt's piano compositions remain among the finest in the repertoire, and his works for orchestra, which he sometimes called symphonic poems, expanded the art form for generations of composers.

Famous Works:

His nineteen *Hungarian Rhapsodies* — for piano
His two *Piano Concertos* — for piano and orchestra
Faust Symphony — for orchestra and voices
Piano Sonata in B minor — for piano
Les Préludes — for orchestra

"You cannot imagine how it spoils one to have been a child prodigy."

Franz Liszt

Gustav Mahler

Goos'-tahf Mahl'-er

born July 7, 1860, Kalischt, Bohemia
(then Austria, now the Czech Republic)
died May 18, 1911, Vienna, Austria

A Composer of the Romantic Era

As a child, Gustav Mahler took piano lessons and showed a great interest in music. His parents took him to the Vienna Conservatory of music, where he was accepted for study at age fifteen. He also studied history and philosophy at the University of Vienna. While at the conservatory from 1875 through 1878, Gustav wrote his first musical compositions. He began work on his first symphony in 1880.

Mahler then began a career as a conductor. Throughout the early 1880s, he took a variety of jobs as orchestra conductor in towns and small cities in Austria, Slovenia, Bohemia, and Germany. In 1885 Mahler was named assistant conductor of the Prague (Czechoslovakia) Opera, and in 1886 became assistant conductor of the Leipzig (Germany) Opera. He later held the position of music director of the Budapest Royal Opera (1888) and conductor of the Hamburg Opera (1891).

By this time, Mahler had established himself as one of the premier orchestral and opera conductors in central Europe. He did most of his composing in the summers, when his orchestras and operas were not performing. In 1897, Mahler became music director of the Vienna State Opera, a very important position. A year later he also took on the position of conductor of the Vienna Philharmonic. Undoubtedly, Mahler was now the most important musical figure in Austria.

In 1901 (age forty), Mahler purchased a summer home near a lake in the Austrian countryside. He used this home as a retreat where he worked on his music. He wrote four symphonies here between 1901 and 1907. Mahler was now composing orchestral music almost exclusively, although some of his symphonies called for singers in addition to a full orchestra. He married Alma Schindler in 1902 and settled into a productive professional life as a composer and conductor. However, after several years with the Vienna Philharmonic and the Vienna State Opera, disagreements with both organizations caused him to resign.

Mahler moved to the United States in 1907 and was named conductor of the Metropolitan Opera. In 1909 (age forty-nine), he added the position of conductor of the New York Philharmonic. Mahler held these positions until 1911, although he continued to spend his summers in Europe. Once again, disagreements and conflicts with his employers caused him to resign. In 1911 he returned to Vienna, where he died of a heart attack in May.

As a conductor, Gustav Mahler was always well received by audiences and music critics. The same cannot be said of his music. During his lifetime, Mahler's symphonies were often considered to be too long, too loud, and too complex. His music fell into disfavor after his death, but were revived later in the twentieth century. Although some of his symphonies were written in the early twentieth century, Mahler is considered the last great composer of the Romantic era.

Famous Works:

His ten symphonies, especially
Symphonies No. 1, 2, and 5.

Symphonies No. 5 through 10 are very difficult, and are performed less frequently than Symphonies No. 1 through 4.

"Only when I experience do I compose — only when I compose do I experience."

Gustav Mahler

Felix Mendelssohn

Feh'-lix Mehn'-dehl-sohn
(He is sometimes referred to as Felix Mendelssohn-Bartholdy.)

born February 3, 1809, Hamburg, Germany
died November 4, 1847, Leipzig, Germany

A Composer of the Romantic Era

Felix Mendelssohn was born to a wealthy family in Hamburg, Germany. When Felix was three, his family moved to Berlin to escape an invading French army. Like his sister Fanny Mendelssohn Hensel, Felix studied piano with his mother and with respected teachers in Berlin. He began giving piano concerts at age ten and composing at twelve. As a teenager, he wrote several symphonies, numerous works for string quartet, and two operas.

At age twenty, Felix began a concert tour of Europe, playing piano and conducting orchestras. On this tour, he met many famous and respected musicians and developed a wide circle of friends throughout Europe.

One of Mendelssohn's teachers owned several copies of works by Johann Sebastian Bach. At this time, Bach's music was not well known. After studying the manuscripts, Mendelssohn believed that Bach's music should be more widely performed. In 1829, he organized a performance of Bach's music, including a choral work known as the *St. Matthew Passion,* and it was a great success. Today the *St. Matthew Passion* is recognized as one of Bach's greatest works, and without Mendelssohn's support it may have been lost.

In 1835 (age twenty-six), he was appointed conductor of an orchestra in Leipzig, Germany. Two years later he married Cecile Jeanrenaud. While in Leipzig, Mendelssohn became more serious about composing. King Wilhelm IV of Bavaria (today a part of Germany) recognized Mendelssohn's musical talents, and in 1840 hired him to become the director of a proposed Academy of the Arts in Berlin. Mendelssohn took the job but the academy was never built. He then returned to Leipzig, although he continued to guest conduct an orchestra for the king in Berlin.

Still another king, in Saxony (also a part of today's Germany), hired Mendelssohn to organize a musical conservatory in 1843 (age thirty-four). This one was built and Mendelssohn made it a success; he was very devoted to music education in Germany. Throughout this period, his life consisted of composing, teaching, and conducting. As a composer, he received many commissions from several European orchestras. He also made several tours of England where he was highly regarded as both a composer and conductor.

By his mid-thirties Mendelssohn's schedule was hectic. He was continually composing, touring, and teaching. He was greatly saddened at the death of his sister Fanny in 1847; he relied greatly on her advice throughout his career. Felix's death at the age of thirty-eight was basically caused by overwork and the sadness of his sister's death.

Felix Mendelssohn was full of charm, enjoyed social events, and had many interests outside of music. He always performed his duties at the conservatory in spite of his busy conducting schedule. He accepted many commissions and worked hard on all of them, no matter how small.

Famous Works:

Overture from A Midsummer Night's Dream — for orchestra
Violin Concerto — for violin and orchestra
Elijah — an oratorio for chorus and orchestra
His five symphonies — for orchestra
Songs without Words — eight collections of compositions for piano

"Music fills the soul with things a thousand times better than words."
Felix Mendelssohn

Claudio Monteverdi

Clow'-dee-oh Mohn-tih-vair'-dee

born May 15, 1567 (date of baptism), Cremona, Italy
died November 29, 1643, Venice, Italy

A Composer of the Renaissance and Baroque Eras

As a child, Claudio Monteverdi sang in the boychoir at the cathedral in Cremona, a city known for its many violin makers. At the cathedral he also studied organ and the viol (a kind of early violin), and took lessons in music theory and harmony. He began composing as a teenager, and by age sixteen had already published a collection of motets (unaccompanied works for choir) and sacred madrigals. Other collections of secular (non-church) madrigals were published in 1587, 1590, and 1592. These were traditional small vocal pieces of the Renaissance era.

When he was twenty-two, Monteverdi married Claudia de Cattaneis, a singer, but she lived for only eight more years. Shortly after the marriage, Monteverdi went to work as a court musician for the court of Mantua, in Italy. Here he wrote his first opera, *La favola d'Orfeo,* in 1607. When his patron, Duke Vincenzo of Mantua, died, Monteverdi left Mantua and became choir director at St. Mark's cathedral in Venice. He remained in this position for thirty years, from 1613 until his death in 1643.

While in Venice, Monteverdi continued to compose music for the Court of Mantua, but most of this music was destroyed during a war in 1630. That same year, he joined the priesthood. Despite his duties to the church and his responsibilities at St. Mark's cathedral, Monteverdi found time to write music for many public events such as weddings, plays, and ballets. He also began to compose vocal music, including madrigals and motets, in a more complex style—more like the Baroque music of Johann Sebastian Bach.

In 1637, the city of Venice built its first great opera house and commissioned Monteverdi, at the age of seventy, to write several operas. They were all well received by audiences. In fact, all his music was extremely popular in Venice. As dramatic works, Monteverdi's operas are frequently compared to the plays of William Shakespeare. Just as Shakespeare transformed drama, Monteverdi transformed opera from a simple staged work with voices to a richer, more dramatic style.

Although Claudio Monteverdi wrote a great deal of music during his seventy-six years, he worked slowly and deliberately. He was always able to adapt to changing tastes and styles, and his music bridges the gap between the Renaissance and Baroque eras. He began by writing simple madrigals for small choral groups and ended by composing operas, cantatas, and other dramatic musical works for voices with orchestral accompaniments. He was one of the first composers to use effects as tremolo and pizzicato in writing for string instruments. Many of Monteverdi's compositions have been lost over the centuries, and there was little interest in his works from his death until the early twentieth century, when his music was rediscovered.

Famous Works:

His nine books of madrigals — for voices
La favola d'Orfeo (The Legend of Orpheus) — an opera
Il Ritorno d'Ulisse in patria
(The Return of Ulysses to His Country) — an opera
L'incoronazione di Poppea (The Coronation of Poppea)
— an opera
Vespro della beata vergine (Vespers for the Blessed Virgin)
— for choir and soloists

"When I make either church or chamber music, I can assure you that the whole city [of Venice] runs to hear it."
Claudio Monteverdi

Wolfgang Amadeus Mozart

Volf'-gahng Ah-mah-day'-oos Moh'-tsart
(In German, a "w " is pronounced like an English "v")

born January 27, 1756, Salzburg, Austria
died December 5, 1791, Vienna, Austria

A Composer of the Classical Era

Encouraged by his father, Leopold, Wolfgang Mozart began playing the clavier (a keyboard instrument like a piano) at the age of four. In less than a year, he began composing, and by age ten Wolfgang had written his first symphony. He could play any music put in front of him on the clavier, organ, or violin. He wrote his first opera at fourteen.

Wolfgang was a child musical prodigy. His father, a violinist, guided Wolfgang's career as a touring concert artist throughout Europe. In addition to presenting his son's talent to huge audiences, Leopold wanted Wolfgang to become familiar with the various styles of music popular throughout Europe.

When they weren't touring, Wolfgang and his father were employed by the Archbishop of Salzburg—Leopold as an orchestra conductor and Wolfgang as a violinist. The archbishop recognized Wolfgang's talent and allowed father and son to take leaves of absence for concert tours. When the archbishop died, his successor ended the concert tours and eventually fired Wolfgang. Leopold remained as orchestra conductor.

In 1781 (age twenty-five), Mozart moved to Vienna, Austria, and become a full-time composer and music teacher. Although several of his compositions had been published, he soon realized that he earned less money as a composer than as a performer. He married in 1782, but his new wife, Constanze, found it difficult to deal with his inability to make money as a composer. She encouraged him to seek a position as a court musician.

He took a job as the private musician to the emperor of Austria in 1787. This gave him a small but steady income. As a court musician, Mozart was required to compose music for many occasions, both for public performances and for private gatherings hosted by the emperor. He continued in this position, composing music for the emperor as well as other musical groups in Vienna, until his death, just four years later at the age of thirty-five. Eventually all the hard work of continuous composing and trying to make money caused his health to fail. He died a very poor, overworked musical genius.

Mozart wrote hundreds of musical works, including symphonies, operas, concertos, oratorios, and solo works for clavier. Most of these works were performed in Vienna with great success. Throughout his life, Mozart never had any difficulty in getting his music performed or published, and it was very much admired and appreciated by audiences in Vienna and throughout Europe.

Wolfgang Amadeus Mozart was a short man with piercing eyes and long hair which he groomed carefully. He was outgoing, always friendly, and enjoyed the company of others. He is considered one of the greatest composers of the eighteenth century. He worked tirelessly as a composer and wrote a huge number of works during his short life.

Famous Works:

The Marriage of Figaro — an opera
His forty-one symphonies — for orchestra
His twenty-one piano concertos
— for piano and orchestra
His twenty-four string quartets
— for two violins, viola, and cello
His keyboard music — for piano

"Melody is the very essence of music.
When I think of a good melody,
I think of a fine race horse."

Wolfgang Amadeus Mozart

Modest Mussorgsky

Moh-dest' Moo-sorg'-ski
(Sometimes his last name is spelled Musorgsky)

born March 21, 1839, Karevo, Russia
died March 28, 1881, St. Petersburg, Russia

A Composer of the Romantic Era

Modest Mussorgsky took piano lessons from his mother when he was a child. His father was a wealthy landowner. At age ten, the family moved to St. Petersburg, Russia, and Modest continued his piano studies with a more advanced teacher. Modest's family wanted him to become an army officer and enrolled him in a military school. After graduation, Modest enlisted in the Russian army.

During his two years in the army, Mussorgsky met many musicians. At this time there was great interest in Russian music, and Russians were justifiably proud of the fine composers which the country had produced. Mussorgsky, too, was interested in music, especially in composing, but he did not consider himself trained to be a composer. At this point, his only experience in music was several years of piano lessons. Nevertheless, the musicians and composers he met in the army encouraged him.

While Mussorgsky was in the army, a composer named Mily Balakirev agreed to give Mussorgsky lessons in music theory. He also studied musical scores by Classical Era composers such as Mozart and Beethoven. Mussorgsky left the military in 1858 (age nineteen), and traveled to Moscow. Here he had a nervous breakdown. He recovered, and by 1860 began composing music. Mussorgsky had little money, however, and within a year he took a job as a government clerk in the Russian Ministry of Transport.

During the 1860s, Mussorgsky completed several songs and short orchestral works. He seemed unable to complete large works. He began to have health problems and his mental state was fragile. Drinking, which had always been a problem for him, even in the army, overtook his life. Though his skill as a composer grew, Mussorgsky sank deeper and deeper into alcoholism.

In 1868 (age twenty-nine), he began work on an opera which he never completed. Two years lager, however, Mussorgsky completed his opera masterpiece, *Boris Godunov.* Twice he submitted it for performance at the St. Petersburg opera and it was turned down both times. Eventually it was performed in 1874. The audience enjoyed it but the critics did not. Even some of Mussorgsky's musician friends were puzzled by the opera.

By 1873 (age thirty-four), Mussorgsky was totally consumed by his alcoholism. He had little money and lived in poverty. He continued to compose during the 1870s, though in 1880 his health forced him to leave his government job. He died a year later at the age of forty-two.

Modest Mussorgsky always considered himself an untrained composer. His musical education was limited. Nevertheless, and in spite of his psychological problems and his alcoholism, he composed very imaginative music which is still enjoyed by audiences today.

Famous Works:

Boris Godunov — an opera
Khovanshchina — an opera
Pictures at an Exhibition — for piano
(later scored for orchestra by others)
Night on the Bare Mountain — for orchestra
Songs and Dances of Death — for voice and piano

"What I project is the melody of life."

Modest Mussorgsky

Giovanni Pierluigi da Palestrina

Jee-oh-vahn'-ee Pear-loo-ee'-jee dah Pahl-ehs-tree'-nah

born 1525 or 1526 (exact date unknown), Palestrina, Italy
died February 2, 1594, Rome, Italy

A Composer of the Renaissance Era

Giovanni Pierluigi da Palestrina took his name from the town, Palestrina, in which he was born. Little is known of his early life, although we know he was listed as a member of a boys choir in Palestrina in 1537. By 1544 he was an organist at a cathedral in Palestrina. In 1547 he married Lucrezia Gori. They had three sons.

In 1550 a bishop from the town of Palestrina was named Pope (Julius III). Julius hired Giovanni as choirmaster for the Cappella Giulia, a kind of training school for choir members of the Sistine Chapel in Rome. The choir also accompanied ceremonies in St. Peter's Basilica within the Vatican. By this time Giovanni had begun composing masses as well as other music required by the church. He dedicated his first book of masses to Julius in 1554. When Julius died in 1585, his successor, Pope Paul IV, replaced Palestrina at the Cappella Giulia. Historians believe that Palestrina was dismissed because he was not a priest and because he had begun to compose some secular, non-church related music.

Between 1555 and 1566, Palestrina conducted choirs at various Catholic churches in Rome and continued to compose music for the church. In 1567, he entered the service of Cardinal Ippolito in Tivoli, near Rome, where he was in charge of all music activities for the Cardinal. The church had recently revised its rules for music. This meant that some of Palestrina's masses could not be performed because they contained words which had been eliminated from the mass. Other of his masses were now unsuitable because some of his masses contained secular (non-church) songs.

On two occasions, Palestrina was offered choirmaster positions outside of Italy, but he rejected both offers because he preferred to stay in Rome.

Palestrina's first book of motets (unaccompanied choral works) was published in 1567. In 1571 he returned to the position of choirmaster at Cappella Giulia in Rome. In the late 1570s, Palestrina's wife and three sons died, and he briefly considered becoming a priest. But he changed his mind and married Virginia Dormoli, a wealthy widow, in 1581. For the rest of his life, he managed her financial and business interests while continuing to compose music. Before he died in 1594, he published sixteen collections of his music.

Palestrina wrote music primarily for the Catholic church, including masses and other choral works often accompanied by organ, although he wrote secular (non-church) vocal and choral music as well. Today, just over 100 of his masses survive, although he probably wrote more than that. He also wrote about 450 motets and over eighty madrigals. He is known today as one of the most important composers of music for the Catholic church.

Famous Works:

Missa Papae Marcelli (Pope Marcellus Mass) — for choir
Missa Assumpta est Maria (Mass for Mary) — for choir
Missa Breva (Short Mass) — for choir
Stabat Mater — a motet for choir
Song of Solomon — a book of twenty-nine choral works

"The first and chief use of music is for the service and praise of God, whose gift it is."
John Playford (1623–1686)

Francis Poulenc

Fran'-sis Poo-lank'

born January 7, 1899, Paris, France
died January 30, 1963, Paris, France

A Composer of the Twentieth Century

Francis Poulenc's father was a wealthy pharmaceutical manufacturer in Paris. His mother was an amateur musician who gave her son piano lessons. When Francis showed musical talent, his parents took him to a more advanced teacher, who gave Francis lessons in both piano and music theory.

Poulenc's first compositions, which he had completed by age eighteen, came to the attention of several French composers who encouraged the young man. Poulenc knew that his training was limited, and he began studying harmony with Charles Koechlin, a respected composer and teacher. He never studied counterpoint or orchestration, however, and many musicians, both then and now, considered Poulenc to be an "instinctive" composer. He was also a fine pianist, though he never pursued this as a career.

In the early 1920s, Poulenc became associated with a group of young French composers known as *Les Six* (The Six). They frequently performed their music in concert together. All of the six had grown up hearing French impressionist music by composers such as Debussy, but came of age at a time when young composers in Europe and the United States were embracing the modern harmonies of the twentieth century. All were greatly influenced by both impressionism and modern harmony.

Because of his family's wealth, Poulenc never had to worry about money and could devote his full attention to composing. Throughout the 1920s, Poulenc produced a great many compositions, including ballets, songs, piano music, and chamber music. Some of it was influenced by jazz. His compositions of this decade were considered lighter and less serious than that of some of his *Les Six* colleagues.

When Poulenc was in his early thirties, the death of a close friend caused him to return to Catholicism, the religion of his childhood. His religion became very important to him, and Poulenc began writing serious sacred music for voices and orchestra. Indeed, all Poulanc's music now became more serious and less frivolous. He began writing in larger forms such as operas and orchestral works, including several concertos. His compositions for organ are among the finest in the repertoire.

Poulenc continued composing until his death in 1963 at age sixty-four. He was not a teacher or a performer. He spent his entire life in Paris, composing music. In the 1920s, Poulenc was considered the "lightest" of *Les Six;* it's unlikely that critics of that era would have predicted great success for him. Yet Poulenc's music grew deeper and more serious as he aged. His music has a simple, yet sophisticated quality, often described as charming, which is greatly appealing to today's concert audiences.

Famous Works:

Concerto in D minor — for two pianos and orchestra
Gloria — for chorus and orchestra
Mass in G — for chorus
Les Mamelles de Tirèsias — an opera
Organ Concerto — for organ and string orchestra

"Above all, do not analyze my music — love it!"
Francis Poulenc

Sergei Prokofiev

Sur'-ghee (soft "g") Pro-koff'-yeff
(His last name is sometimes spelled Prokofieff)

born April 27, 1891, Sontsovka, Russia
died March 5, 1953, Moscow, Russia

A Composer of the Twentieth Century

Sergei Prokofiev was born into a wealthy family. His mother gave him piano lessons and arranged for him to study music composition while he was still a child. At age nine, Sergei composed an opera for children. He enrolled at the St. Petersburg Conservatory of music at age thirteen, and by the time he was sixteen, Sergei had written three more operas and a work for orchestra.

When Sergei was nineteen, his father died, and he needed to earn a living. He promptly wrote a piano concerto which was immediately published and premiered in Moscow. In 1914 (age twenty-three), he graduated from the conservatory, winning a prize for his performance of his piano concerto which he performed at a graduation concert.

Compositionally, Prokofiev was already quite advanced. Even as a young man, he wrote music that was dissonant, rhythmic, and powerful—sometimes too dissonant for audiences and critics. Shortly after graduating from the conservatory, Prokofiev wrote a ballet for the famous Russian ballet company, Ballets Russes. He completed his first symphony in 1917, the year of the Russian Revolution. Three years later (age twenty-nine) he moved to Paris.

In Paris, Prokofiev re-established his relationship with Ballets Russes, which had also moved to Paris after the Revolution, and wrote several more ballets. He toured the United States in 1921 to attend the premiere of an opera commissioned by the Chicago Opera Company, *The Love for Three Oranges*. As one biographer put it: "Prokofiev did not care for America and America did not care for him." He continued to live in Paris until the mid 1930s, although he spent a little over a year in the Bavarian region of Germany, where he completed several major works. In the late 1920s, Prokofiev toured Russia several times, as a pianist performing his own music.

Throughout the early 1930s, Prokofiev scheduled more and more of his premieres and performances in Russia. In 1936 (age forty-five), he returned there to live. It was not a good time to be a composer in Russia, however. The government was not receptive to the modern style of music which Prokofiev wrote. For the next decade, Prokofiev composed in a more traditional style which was acceptable to the government. Nevertheless, in 1948, five years before his death, the Russian government condemned Prokofiev for his music.

Sergei Prokofiev began his career as a forward-thinking, progressive composer, very much a part of the new breed of twentieth century composers. As he aged, his music became somewhat more melodic, and at the end, he censored his music to satisfy his critics within the Russian government. He created a large body of work, including music for virtually every genre including choral music, opera, ballets, piano music, and symphonic works.

Famous Works:

Scythian Suite — for orchestra
Peter and the Wolf — for narrator and orchestra
The Love for Three Oranges — an opera
Romeo and Juliet — a ballet
His seven symphonies — for orchestra

"I care nothing for politics.
I'm a composer first and last."
Sergei Prokofiev

Giacomo Puccini

Jhee-ah'-coh-moh Poo-chee'-nee

born December 22, 1858, Lucca, Italy,
died November 29, 1924, Brussels, Belgium

A Composer of the Romantic Era

Giacomo Puccini's father was a composer who died when Giacomo was five. Giacomo then began taking music lessons from his uncle, but showed little interest or talent. His mother, however, was determined to develop Giacomo's musical skills, so she sent him to a local institute of music. Here, Giacomo became a fine student. By the time he was fourteen he was a talented pianist and organist, good enough to serve as a church organist.

When he was eighteen, Giocomo saw a performance of the opera *Aida* by Giuseppe Verdi. He was so impressed by the performance that he decided to become an opera composer. However, Giocomo knew he would have to continue his musical studies in order to develop his skills. In 1880 (age twenty-two), he applied for and received a scholarship to study composition at the Milan Conservatory of music. By the time he completed his studies at the conservatory, three years later, he was writing music which was praised by his teachers as well as concert audiences in Milan.

Puccini's first opera, a short work entitled *Le Villi*, came to the attention of Giuseppe Verdi's publisher, who commissioned Puccini to write a full-length opera. This opera, entitled *Edgar*, was a failure (Puccini called it "a mistake"), but the publisher continued to support and encourage him. Finally, in 1893 (age thirty-five), Puccini completed his first successful opera, *Manon Lescaut*. His next opera, *La Bohème*, was not successful when it was first produced in 1896, but has since become one of the most popular and beloved operas ever written.

La Bohème was followed by another opera, *Tosca*, a huge success. By 1900 (age forty-two), Puccini had become a famous and wealthy man. He built a huge villa in the town of Torre del Lago in the Italian province of Tuscany. His 1904 opera, *Madama Butterfly*, was unsuccessful when it was first produced. But Puccini revised the opera and produced it again, this time to great success. Today both *Tosca* and *Madama Butterfly* are among the most widely performed operas in the world. Puccini traveled to the United States in 1907 (age forty-nine) for the first American performance of *Madama Butterfly*.

By this time, Puccini was recognized as the greatest living opera composer. When he wasn't composing, he spent his days at his Tuscan villa, often duck hunting. He was always on the lookout for a good libretto (the dialog of an opera) which he could set to music. Many of his operas had female heroines whose flawed character resulted in an early death.

Although he never married, Puccini enjoyed the company of beautiful women. In his later life, he enjoyed riding in fast cars and fast motorboats. He became a wealthy man because of his success as an opera composer; when he died, his estate was worth four million dollars. Puccini's music was rather conservative for its time, and he did not embrace the musical changes of the early twentieth century. His operas, however, are widely performed and remain popular.

Famous Works:

Manon Lescaut — an opera.
La Bohème — an opera
Tosca — an opera
Madama Butterfly — an opera
Turandot — an opera

"Almighty God touched me with his little finger and said, 'Write for the theater—only for the theater.' And I have obeyed his supreme command."

Giocomo Puccini

Sergei Rachmaninoff

Ser'-ghee (soft "g") Rahk-mah'-nee-noff
(Sometimes his last name is spelled Rachmaninov or Rakhmaninov)

born April 1, 1873, Semyonovo, Russia
died March 28, 1943, Beverly Hills, California

A Composer of the Twentieth Century

Sergei Rachmaninoff came from a family of amateur musicians, and as a child he took piano lessons from his mother. In 1882, the Rachmaninoff family moved to St. Petersburg, Russia, and Sergei enrolled at the St. Petersburg Conservatory. He was just nine years old. A few years later his parents separated, and Sergei began studying at the Moscow Conservatory. Here he had outstanding teachers who schooled him in piano and composition. He graduated from the conservatory in 1891 (age eighteen).

The same year he graduated, Rachmaninoff completed his first piano concerto, and a year later he finished an opera. Also in 1892 he published a prelude for piano, which quickly became one of the most popular piano works in Europe. Rachmaninoff also began performing as a pianist and as a conductor. In 1897, he completed his first symphony, but the premiere was a disaster. This so disappointed Rachmaninoff that he underwent hypnosis to treat his depression.

His second piano concerto was premiered, with much more success, in 1901 (age twenty-eight), with Rachmaninoff at the piano. The next year he married Natalya Satina. After spending a few more years conducting Russian orchestras, Rachmaninoff moved to Dresden, Germany. Here he completed several major works including a symphony and another piano concerto. For several years he composed in the summer and toured as a performer/conductor in the winter. Rachmaninoff toured the United States in 1909 (age thirty-six) conducting his music. The tour was so successful that he was offered the position of conductor of the Boston Symphony Orchestra. But he declined and returned to Russia.

Rachmaninoff and his family fled to the United States after the Russian Revolution of 1917. They eventually settled in California, where Rachmaninoff lived for the rest of his life. He wrote less after his move to the United States, and very little after 1926 (age fifty-three), when his *Fourth Piano Concerto* was premiered, with little success. His 1934 orchestral composition, *Rhapsody on a Theme of Paganini,* was one of his finest works, however. Rachmaninoff seemed to realize that twentieth century music had somehow passed him by, that he was writing music of the Romantic era in an age of more modern and progressive music.

Sergei Rachmaninoff wrote a great variety of music, though not all of it was successful. He wrote three operas which are rarely performed. But his orchestral works and, especially, his piano music remain quite popular today. He was a physically large and tall man, with huge hands, which obviously is an advantage for a pianist. As a pianist, Rachmaninoff was one of the most outstanding performers of his era, a time when the world was blessed with many fine pianists.

Famous Works:

His three symphonies — for orchestra
His preludes for piano
Piano Concerto No. 4 — for piano and orchestra
Rhapsody on a Theme of Paganini — for orchestra
The Isle of the Dead — for orchestra

"I cannot cast out the old way of writing and I cannot acquire the new."
Sergei Rachmaninoff

Maurice Ravel

Maw-rees' Rah-vell'

born March 7, 1875, Ciboure, France
died December 28, 1937 Paris, France

A Composer of the Twentieth Century

When Maurice Ravel was a baby, his parents moved from a small town to Paris, France, where Maurice lived for his entire life. He began taking piano lessons at age seven and entered the Paris Conservatory of music in 1889 (age fourteen). He studied at the conservatory until 1895. By then Maurice had completed his first compositions, mostly for piano.

Ravel returned to the conservatory in 1897 and studied with composer Gabriel Fauré. While studying with Fauré he completed several advanced orchestral works. By this time Ravel had already developed his own unique musical style using unusual harmonies, even though his music was based on traditional forms of the Classical and Romantic eras. His style falls into what is known as "Impressionistic," creating a soft musical picture, just as Impressionistic painters use soft colors to convey the impression of a scene.

While in his twenties, Ravel became very interested in literature and poetry, which led him to compose songs set to the works of famous poets. By 1905 (age thirty), Ravel was established as a famous composer in France, and was a popular figure in Paris society. He became a member of a group of French poets, artists, and musicians known as *Les Apaches*. He was now totally devoted to developing his talents as a composer, and continued to write more orchestral works and ballets. In 1907 he began work on his first opera, *L'heure espagnole (The Spanish Hour)*.

When World War I broke out in Europe in 1914, Ravel attempted, at the age of thirty-nine, to enlist in the French army. When he was rejected because of his small build, he became an ambulance driver. After the war he portrayed its horrors in an orchestral work, *La Valse (The Waltz)*. He also wrote several works which he dedicated to friends who had died in battle. And when famous French composer Claude Debussy died in 1918, Ravel dedicated to him a duo for violin and piano.

His next major work was the 1925 opera, *L'enfant et les sortiléges (The Child and the Magic Spells)*, in which he created a magical world of talking toys and animals. Ravel visited the United States in 1928 (age fifty-three). The same year he composed a ballet entitled *Boléro*, which has become one of his most popular works. In the early 1930s, he wrote two important piano concertos, including one in which the pianist plays only with his left hand. This piece was written for a pianist who had lost his right arm in World War I. In the last five years of his life, Ravel suffered from poor health as a result of a brain injury he received in an automobile accident. He underwent brain surgery in December, 1937, and died a few days later at the age of sixty-two.

Maurice Ravel was a physically small man who wore elegant clothes and was very popular in the clubs and societies of early twentieth century Paris. He made a living exclusively by writing music. He rarely conducted his music, and never held a teaching position, although he occasionally gave private lessons in composition.

Famous Works:

Daphnis et Chloé (Daphnis and Chloé) — a ballet
Gaspard de la Nuit (Demons of the Night) — for piano
Boléro (1928) — a ballet, and later an orchestral work
Le Tombeau de Couperin — for piano
His piano concertos, especially numbers 2 and 3 — for piano and orchestra

"I think and feel in sounds."
Maurice Ravel

Gioacchino Rossini

Gee-oh-ah-chee'-noh Roh-see'-nee

born February 29, 1792, Pesaro, Italy
died November 13, 1868, Paris, France

A Composer of the Classical Era

Both of Gioacchino Rossini's parents were musicians; his father was a trumpeter and his mother an opera singer. Gioacchino learned to play the harpsichord and sang in churches as a child. He entered a music school in Bologna, Italy, at age fourteen. In school he showed great talent, frequently winning awards and prizes. Soon Gioacchino had written his first opera.

Within a span of two years, from 1810 through 1811, he wrote six more operas, one of which was commissioned by the famous La Scala opera house in Milan, Italy. An important opera manager, Domenico Barbaja, was impressed by these operas and offered Rossini an exclusive contract. Rossini accepted and agreed to compose two operas a year. Apparently writing came easy to him; he claimed none of his operas took more than a few weeks to write.

To this point, most of Rossini's operas were serious, dramatic works, known to Italians as *opera seria*. But he was determined to compose comic opera *(opera buffa)* as well. His most famous comic opera was *Il barbiere di Siviglia (The Barber of Seville)*, written in 1816.

Its opening night, in Rome, was a failure, because of several disasters and accidents on stage. It was also poorly received because audiences compared it unfavorably to an opera of the same name by another popular opera composer. But today, *The Barber of Seville* is recognized as one of the greatest Italian comic operas ever written. Rossini was just twenty-four years old when he composed it.

Rossini wrote sixteen more operas in the next six years. For the next several years, he traveled throughout Italy composing operas which were produced in important opera houses. At one point he settled in Vienna, Austria, where he was hailed as an operatic genius. He stayed only four months before returning to Italy. In 1824 (age thirty-two) Rossini moved to Paris. Here, two years later, he entered into a contract which called for him to compose five new operas over the next ten years.

The first and only opera Rossini completed under this contract was *Guillaume Tell (William Tell)*, which was a great success when it opened in Paris in 1829. It would be Rossini's last opera. He was only thirty-seven years old. After that, he wrote only a few pieces of sacred music, including one of his most famous, *Stabat Mater.*

There are many theories why Gioacchino Rossini abandoned composing operas at the height of his creative success. He was wealthy, and claimed to be lazy. Yet, laziness is not a character trait of a man who once composed sixteen operas in six years. He was involved in legal battles, he was frustrated at finding first rate singers to perform his operas, and his health was in decline. And he was concerned with political events in Europe. Yet none of these reasons fully explain why Gioacchino Rossini, one of the greatest of all opera composers, didn't write an opera during the last forty years of his life.

Famous Works:

Il barbiere di Siviglia (The Barber of Seville) — an opera
Guillaume Tell (William Tell) — an opera
Otello — an opera
Stabat Mater — for chorus and orchestra
L'Italiana in Algeri (The Italian Woman in Algiers) —
an overture for orchestra adapted from
one of his operas

"Give me a laundry list and I'll set it to music!"
Gioacchino Rossini

Arnold Schoenberg

His last name is pronounced Shown'-berg (first syllable rhymes with "own")

born September 13, 1874, Vienna, Austria
died July 13, 1951, Los Angeles, California

A Composer of the Twentieth Century

Arnold Schoenberg's parents encouraged their son's interest in music, and Arnold began taking violin lessons at age eight. When Arnold was fifteen, his father died. Arnold left school and took a job as a bank clerk. He studied music in the evenings and, in addition to the violin, learned to play the cello.

In 1901, Arnold married Mathilde Zemlinsky. Mathilde's brother, Alexander, was a musician, and Arnold began to take composition lessons from his brother-in-law. He had already composed several works, including a string quartet. He was, however, unsatisfied with these early works. They were, he felt, too much influenced by composers of the late Romantic era. Arnold wanted to push the limits of harmony, and felt limited by the style and harmonies of Romantic music.

Arnold and Mathilde soon moved to Berlin where he supported his family by arranging popular music for cabaret singers, and by teaching at a school of music. Eventually Schoenberg developed a compositional style in which he used the musical forms and structure of the Classical era, but pushed his musical tonalities well beyond that of either the Classical or Romantic eras. In fact, by 1907 he began to abandon traditional musical tonalities entirely. These compositions were known as atonal, and were not well received by concert audiences. One example of Schoenberg's innovations was a style of speech singing known as *Sprechtstimme.*

Schoenberg returned to Vienna in 1915 (age forty-one). He enlisted in the German army, and served briefly, but was discharged because of poor health. After World War I, he founded the Society for Private Musical Performances in Vienna. For several years, the society presented performances of new music by Schoenberg, his colleagues, and students. By the early 1920s, Schoenberg had abandoned traditional harmony altogether in favor of what he called twelve-note, or twelve-tone, style. This style of composition utilized all twelve notes within a musical octave equally, as opposed to focusing only on certain notes within a specific key. His first important twelve-tone piece was his *Five Piano Pieces.*

His wife, Mathilde, died in 1923, and a year later he married Gertrude Kolisch. From 1925 until 1933, Schoenberg taught at an arts academy in Berlin. Here he composed many of his most important works. In 1933 (age fifty-nine), with the rise of Nazi Germany, Schoenberg moved to France and, ultimately, the United States. He settled in California where he befriended composer George Gershwin and taught at the University of California, Los Angeles, as well as the University of Southern California. In 1947 (age seventy-three), he was elected to membership in the American Academy of Arts and Letters.

Arnold Schoenberg's music was revolutionary, and not always appreciated by audiences during his lifetime. Today, however, he is recognized as an important musical innovator of the twentieth century.

Famous Works:

Piano Concerto — for piano and orchestra
Chamber Symphony No. 1 — for orchestra
Five Piano Pieces
Moses and Aron — an opera
Theme and Variations for Orchestra

"If it is art it is not for all, and if it is for all it is not art."
Arnold Schoenberg

Franz Schubert

Frahnts Shoo'-beart

born January 31, 1797, Vienna, Austria
died November 19, 1828, Vienna Austria

A Composer of the Classical Era

Franz Schubert's father was a schoolteacher, and everyone in the Schubert family enjoyed and played music. Franz received music lessons from his father and his older brothers. As a child, he attended a boychoir school where he sang in the choir and played violin in the orchestra. He began to compose while he was a student.

The boychoir school gave Franz an excellent musical education. After graduation at age seventeen, he taught music at the same school where his father taught. He now began to spend his evenings composing. He wrote rapidly, not caring whether or not his music would ever be performed. After two years, he left this teaching position and moved in with friends to devote nearly all of his time to composing. He had virtually no income and began neglecting his health by eating poorly and sleeping very little.

Eventually, Schubert realized he needed a steady source of income. In 1818 (age twenty-one), he took a job as music teacher at the summer home of Count Esterhazy—the same count who supported the composer Franz Joseph Haydn. Here Schubert made many influential friends and met many important court musicians and composers who could have been helpful in getting his music performed. But he was unable to develop these friendships and most of his music remained unperformed outside the Esterhazy palace. Count Esterhazy offered him the position of court organist, but Schubert declined because he didn't like the schedule. He resigned after just two years.

By age twenty-three, he had written over 500 musical works, but only two had ever been performed in public. For several years he spent his mornings composing, his afternoons with friends, and his nights partying. He was always short of money and lived in terrible conditions. His health began to fail.

In March of 1828, friends put together a concert devoted exclusively to Schubert's music. It was well received by the audience and critics; his friends told him success was near. Unfortunately, he died eight months later at the age of thirty-one.

Ten years after Schubert's death, another composer, Robert Schumann, began studying Schubert's music and organized performances of his orchestral music. The performances were very successful and created tremendous interest in Schubert's music. One of his most famous works is his *Symphony No. 8*. It was unfinished at the time of his death, and eventually became known as the *Unfinished Symphony*. It was not performed until thirty-seven years after his death. Other symphonies were discovered and performed much later.

Writing music was Franz Schubert's only goal in life. He had no business sense and lived in poverty for most of his adult life. He composed rapidly and didn't care about the value of his music or whether or not it would ever be performed.

Famous Works:

Symphony No. 8 ("Unfinished Symphony") — for orchestra
Piano Quintet in A — for piano, violin, viola, cello, and bass
String Quartet No. 14 — for two violins, viola, and cello
His songs — there are more than 600
Fantasy in C Major — for piano

"I have come into the world for no purpose but to compose."

Franz Schubert

Clara Schumann

Her last name is pronounced Shoo'-mahn
(Her maiden name was Clara Wieck, pronounced Veek.)

born September 13, 1819, Leipzig, Germany
died May 20, 1896, Frankfurt, Germany

A Composer of the Romantic Era

Clara Wieck's father, Friedrich Wieck, was a famous piano teacher in the German city of Leipzig. Naturally, Clara became one of her father's students, and Friedrich developed a special method for teaching his daughter music theory, composition, and counterpoint, in addition to piano, voice, and violin. By age eleven, Clara was an accomplished pianist, and her father took her on a concert tour of Europe. She had her first compositions, all piano music, published at age thirteen.

In 1830, Clara's father began teaching a twenty year old piano student named Robert Schumann. Seven years later, when Clara was eighteen, Robert asked Clara to marry him. Clara's father was violently opposed to their marriage, and at one point threatened to kill Robert if he continued to see Clara. Eventually Robert filed a lawsuit to permit the couple to be married. It was granted and they wed in 1840.

The couple moved first to Dresden, Germany, then to Düsseldorf, and finally back to Leipzig. Clara continued performing and touring as a pianist while she raised her children. She also taught piano at the Leipzig Conservatory of music and composed. When Robert Schumann died in 1856, Clara moved to Berlin where she lived until 1878. She continued her concert tours with performances in England and Russia.

After her husband's death, Clara befriended many fine young composers, such as Johannes Brahms, and encouraged them in their work. In fact, Clara and Brahms fell in love, although they never married. She also spent many years carefully editing her husband's music for his publisher, and never missed an opportunity to promote his music.

In 1878 (age fifty-nine), Clara settled in Frankfurt, Germany and taught at the Hoch Conservatory of music. She held this position until 1892 (age seventy-three). In her concert tours, which continued until 1891, she frequently performed her late husband's music and occasionally her own. Throughout her career, Clara was highly regarded as a piano teacher, and she attracted outstanding students from throughout Europe.

During Clara Schumann's lifetime, composing music was considered a job for men. And although Clara had done some composing as a teenager, she cut back on her writing after her marriage to Robert. Still, even though her husband demanded complete silence in the house when he was composing, Clara managed to complete many successful works during the marriage. She wrote mostly songs and music for piano, with some orchestral and chamber pieces. Her music is performed more frequently today than it was during her lifetime.

Clara composed very little after Robert's death. Her music was similar to her husband's music: conservative, straightforward, and melodic. In fact, Robert used several of Clara's melodies in his own compositions.

Famous Works:

Piano Concerto — for piano and orchestra
Many works for piano
Drei Romanzen — for violin and piano
Piano Trio — for piano, violin, and cello

"Composing gives me great pleasure. There is nothing that surpasses the joy of creation."

Clara Schumann

Robert Schumann

His last name is pronounced Shoo'-mahn

born June 8, 1810, Zwickau, Germany
died July 29, 1856, Endenich, near Bonn, Germany

A Composer of the Romantic Era

Robert Schumann's father was an author and publisher who taught his son to love books and reading. Robert developed an interest in music when he began taking piano lessons at age six. As a young man, he attended law school but often neglected his studies to attend concerts and take piano lessons. At first, Robert considered a career as a concert pianist and took piano lessons from a famous teacher, Friedrich Wieck. However, Robert developed a physical problem with one of his fingers. This ended his dream of becoming a concert pianist.

Robert's father died when Robert was sixteen, and his mother pleaded with her son to continue his law studies. But Robert was determined to become a musician. With his piano career ended, he became interested in composing, and began to study composition with respected teachers. His first composition, *Abegg Variations*, was based on the musical notes A, B, E, G, and G. At first he focused on piano music, then began to write songs, which he set to famous poetry.

In 1833 (age twenty-three), he helped organize a musical society to encourage composers to write what he called "progressive" new music. A few years later he fell in love with Clara Wieck, the daughter of his former piano teacher, Friedrich Wieck. Friedrich opposed his daughter's relationship with Robert, and, at one point, threatened to kill Robert if he continued to see Clara. Robert stayed away from Clara for four years. Eventually, Robert filed a lawsuit to permit the couple to be married. It was granted, and they wed in 1840.

Clara was an outstanding pianist and performed many of Schumann's early compositions. Schumann wanted to write "progressive music." But Clara, who was well-schooled in the music of the masters, such as Bach and Mozart, pushed him toward a less contemporary, more classical style.

In the early 1840s, Schumann had moved beyond piano music and songs, and was concentrating on orchestral and chamber music. He and Clara moved to Leipzig, Germany, where he taught taught piano and composition at a music conservatory. Health problems caused him to resign and concentrate on composition. He completed his *Symphony in C Major* in 1846.

In 1850 Schumann took a conducting position in Düsseldorf, Germany, but was a failure. Once again, he left his job to concentrate on composing. By this time, however, Schumann was very depressed with his life. He tried to commit suicide by jumping into a river, and in 1854 was placed in an insane asylum where he remained until he died two years later at age forty-six

Robert Schumann was a handsome man, of moderate height and build, who was self-centered and absent-minded. He was poor at self-promotion, and perhaps for that reason his music was not well received during his lifetime. Schumann's wife, Clara, outlived him by forty years and she continued to promote his music after his death.

Famous Works:

His four symphonies — for orchestra
Piano Concerto — for piano and orchestra
His songs (about 250)
His piano music, including
Carnaval and *Fantasie in C*

"In order to compose, all you need do is remember a tune that no one else has thought of."
Robert Schumann

Dmitri Shostakovich

Da-mee'-tree Shaws-ta-koh'-vitch

born September 25, 1906, St. Petersburg, Russia
died August 9, 1975, Moscow, Russia

A Composer of the Twentieth Century

Dmitri Shostakovich's father was an engineer and his mother a professional pianist. Although Dmitri showed musical talent as a young child, his mother waited until Dmitri was nine before starting him on the piano. He progressed quickly, and at the age of thirteen entered the conservatory of music in what is now St. Petersburg, Russia. As a graduation project, Dmitri composed his first symphony. It was premiered in 1926 to great success and made Dmitri famous. He was just twenty years old.

After graduation, Shostakovich continued his post-graduate studies in composition. His father had died and Shostakovich had little money. To support himself, he gave piano recitals, sometimes playing his own music. He was good enough to win an honorable mention at a piano competition in Paris. In Paris, Shostakovich met German conductor Bruno Walter, who encouraged Shostakovich, and conducted Shostakovich's *First Symphony* in Berlin. Inspired by Walter, Shostakovich now devoted all his time to composing, particularly large symphonic works and operas. In 1927 (age twenty-one), he was commissioned by the Russian Communist Party to write a symphony to celebrate the tenth anniversary of the Russian Revolution.

Shostakovich achieved great success in Russia in the 1930s. His music was becoming more creative and original, and less influenced by Russian folk music. In 1936 (age thirty), after a Moscow performance of Shostakovich's opera *Lady Macbeth of Mtsensk*, Russian government officials denounced his music as "degenerate." Suddenly, Shostakovich had lost favor with the Communist government. He was distraught and returned to his earlier, more conservative style with his *Fifth Symphony*, which returned him to favor with the government. During the late 1930s and 1940s he completed numerous film scores, ballets, concertos, and orchestral works. Many of these works became popular around the world. His *Seventh Symphony*, written in Leningrad in 1941 (age thirty-five), during the German siege of that city, made him a Russian hero.

In 1948 (age forty-one), Shostakovich, along with several other Russian composers, was again condemned by the Communist Party for writing "discordant" music. Still, Shostakovich and his colleagues continued to compose. Throughout the entire period of his problems with the government, Shostakovich remained extremely popular with the Russian public. By 1957, the Russian government had relaxed its policies toward music, and Shostakovich was elected an officer of the Union of Soviet Composers. In 1966 (age sixty), the Russian government awarded him its highest civillian honor.

No government could stifle Dmitri Shostakovich's creativity. His life was marked by alternating praise and condemnation from the Russian government, which caused him a great deal of anguish. In the end, his music was all that mattered. During a career which lasted nearly fifty years, Shostakovich produced a huge number of compositions in many different performing mediums.

Famous Works:

His fourteen symphonies — for orchestra
Lady Macbeth of Mtsensk — an opera
The Bolt — a ballet
His string quartets, especially
String Quartet No. 2 — for two violins, viola, and cello

"There were no particularly happy moments in my life. It was gray and dull, and it makes me sad to think about it."

Dmitri Shostakovich, in his memoirs

John Philip Sousa

(His last name is pronounced Soo'-sah)

born November 6, 1854, Washington, DC
died March 6, 1932, Reading, Pennsylvania

A Composer of the Romantic Era and the Twentieth Century

John Philip Sousa attended public schools in the District of Columbia and took music lessons at a private music school. His father was a member of the United States Marine Band. As a teenager, John enlisted in the Marines and served as an apprentice musician in the Marine Band until the age of twenty. As an apprentice, he studied theory, harmony, and composition. He also took lessons on the violin, his primary instrument.

After leaving the Marine Band, Sousa toured as a conductor of musical theater productions. In 1876 he moved to Philadelphia where he played violin in an orchestra at the American Centennial celebration. Here he began to compose music.

In 1880 (age twenty-six), Sousa was named conductor of the United States Marine Band, a position he held for twelve years. He then resigned his military commission and formed his own band which he called Sousa's Band. Every year for the rest of his life, he spent from six to twelve months on tour throughout the United States with Sousa's Band.

As leader of Sousa's Band, John Philip Sousa was one of the most recognized musicians in the world. He was a great showman, always requiring the utmost professionalism from his band members. During World War I, he temporarily disbanded Sousa's Band, re-enlisted in the Navy, and formed a 300 member band of sailors which toured throughout the United States. After the war he took up a touring schedule once again with Sousa's Band.

Sousa is best known for the 136 marches he wrote for his band. He also composed seventy songs, several extended suites for band, as well as numerous waltzes and dance pieces for band. For the concert stage, he composed several operas and operettas. The operettas, in particular, were well liked by audiences. He also arranged more than a hundred orchestral works for band.

For the first two decades of the twentieth century, John Philip Sousa had a significant impact on the business of music. His band tours generated a steady income, and his marches, which were published in editions for band as well as piano, sold well. And recordings of Sousa's Band were among the first top sellers for the new recording industry. He continued touring and guest conducting bands throughout the United States until his death.

No one was more influential in developing bands in the United States than John Philip Sousa. His band tours exposed millions of Americans to a highly professional musical ensemble, and many of his band members went on to found and conduct bands throughout the country. To this day, his marches are considered the finest examples of the form and are still widely performed by bands around the world.

Famous Works:

Semper Fidelis — a march for band
Manhattan Beach March — for band
Stars and Stripes Forever — a march for band
The Liberty Bell — a march for band
El Capitan — an operetta

*"I can almost always write music;
at any hour of the twenty-four,
if I put pencil to paper, music comes."*

John Philip Sousa

Richard Strauss

Pronounce in the German manner, Rikh'-art Strous (rhymes with "blouse")

born June 11, 1864, Munich, Germany
died September 8, 1949,
Germisch-Partenkirchen, Germany

A Composer of the Romantic Era

Richard Strauss's father was perhaps the most famous horn player in Germany. Young Richard took lessons on piano and violin. He later said that he began composing and improvising at the piano while still a boy. Richard wrote his first symphony at the age of seventeen, and it was premiered in Munich. A second symphony followed three years later.

When Richard graduated from high school, he entered the University of Munich, where he took some courses but never worked toward a degree. After a year, he left school and moved to Berlin, where he managed to get a few orchestras to perform his music. A famous conductor, Hans von Bülow of the Meiningen Orchestra, was impressed with Strauss's music and gave him several commissions to write orchestral works. Within a few years von Bülow named Strauss as associate conduction of the Meiningen Orchestra, and eventually as principal conductor. He also performed frequently as a pianist with the orchestra.

Strauss now had three careers: composer, conductor, and concert pianist. Because the Meiningen Orchestra would perform anything he wrote, Strauss concentrated on large symphonic works. His orchestras often performed the music of composers such as Berlioz, and Wagner. Because their music was very progressive, it came to be known as the "Music of the Future." Though he was considerably younger than Berlioz and Wagner, Strauss composed music that definitely was not "of the future." It was more melodic and rooted in the forms of the Classical era. But he listened to the music of other composers with an open mind, and ever so slightly began moving his music in a more contemporary direction. Never, however, would Strauss's music be called "Modern."

In 1886, Strauss became conductor of the Munich Opera. He was still only twenty-two years old. Here he met his future wife, Pauline de Ahna, an opera singer; they married in 1894 (age thirty). Throughout the 1890s, he wrote several orchestral tone poems, a new musical form in which music develops or expresses an idea from another medium, such as a poem, a story, or a painting. In 1898 he became conductor of the Berlin Royal Opera, and in the early 1900s he focused on composing operas.

Strauss remained at the Berlin opera until 1918 (age fifty-four) when he was appointed joint director of the Vienna Opera in Austria. Throughout this period he was in constant demand as a conductor throughout Europe. After 1920 Strauss began to concentrate on smaller works such as songs, though he completed a short opera in 1938.

Richard Strauss was a composer who outlived his era. He was influenced by the "Modern" music of Berlioz and Wagner, but he never pushed tonality and harmony as much as they did. And although he lived nearly fifty years into the twentieth century, it certainly cannot be said that his music incorporated many of the traits of modern, twentieth century music.

Famous Works:

Also Sprach Zarathustra — a tone poem for orchestra
Don Juan — a tone poem for orchestra
Symphony in F minor — a tone poem for orchestra
Salome — an opera
Der Rosenkavalier — an opera

"There is no such thing as Abstract music; there is good music and bad music. If it is good, it means something."

Richard Strauss

Igor Stravinsky

Ee'-gor Strah-vin'-skee

born June 17, 1882, Oranienbaum
(today Lomonosov), Russia
died April 6, 1971, New York, New York

A Composer of the Twentieth Century

Igor Stravinsky's father was a singer with an opera company. After the family moved to St. Petersburg, Russia, Igor attended his father's opera performances. He began piano lessons at nine. In spite of Igor's musical talent, his parents wanted him to become a lawyer rather than a musician. Igor spent several semesters studying law at the University of St. Petersburg. But he also continued his music studies, including composition lessons with a well-known Russian composer, Nicolai Rimsky-Korsakov.

Stravinsky much preferred music to the practice of law but wasn't sure he could make a living as a musician. Nevertheless, upon graduation and marriage to Catherine Nosenko, he embarked upon a career in music. In 1908, his first symphony was performed. He was twenty-six. His symphony came to the attention of the director of the Ballet Russe, a famous ballet company. The Ballet Russe commissioned Stravinsky to write several works for his company. A number of these ballet suites, including *The Firebird* and *Petrouchka,* were performed with much success.

In 1913, the premiere of one of Stravinsky's most famous orchestral works, *The Rite of Spring,* nearly caused a riot in the concert hall. The work was very different from what concert audiences were used to hearing. In fact, many in the audience did not even consider it music! In 1919 (age thirty-seven), Stravinsky moved to Paris, France, and continued to write ballets for the Ballet Russe. He eventually became a French citizen. He would not return to Russia for over forty years. Between 1925 and 1939 he traveled several times to the United States, conducting performances of his music.

Because of war in Europe and the death of his wife, Stravinsky moved to the United States and settled in Massachusetts in 1939 (age fifty-seven). He remarried in 1940, became a United States citizen in 1945, and moved to California where he lived for the rest of his life. To celebrate his new citizenship, he wrote an orchestral arrangement of *The Star Spangled Banner*.

After moving to California, Stravinsky began taking commissions from a variety of sources, including the Ringling Bros. Circus, a jazz band, and an opera company. He continued to compose ballets. In 1962 (age eighty), he returned to Russia for the first time since 1919, and was welcomed by Russian concert audiences. In his final years, he wrote fewer large orchestral works and more shorter works for smaller groups of instruments

Igor Stravinsky was neat and precise. These traits were apparent in his musical scores, which were very well crafted and carefully written. No matter where he lived, Stravinsky's composing routine varied little. He planned each day carefully. Mornings were spent in his office writing music. Afternoons were devoted to office work and correspondence. Throughout his life, Stravinsky ignored the opinions, advice, and suggestions of others regarding his music, and did not seem to care whether or not critics or audiences liked his music.

Famous Works:

The Firebird — a ballet
Symphony of Psalms — for chorus and chamber group of mostly wind instruments
Symphony in Three Movements — for orchestra
The Rake's Progress — an opera
The Rite of Spring — a ballet

"Rhythm and motion, not the element of feeling, are the foundations of musical art."
Igor Stravinsky

Peter Ilyich Tchaikovsky

Pee'-tur Il-yetch' Chi-koff'-skee
(His first name is sometimes spelled Piotr.)

born May 7, 1840, Votkinsk, Russia
died November 6, 1893, St. Petersburg, Russia

A Composer of the Romantic Era

Peter Ilyich Tchaikovsky did not begin studying music seriously until the age of twenty-two. Until then, he had only taken a few piano lessons. After graduating from preparatory school, he became a clerk in the Russian Ministry of Justice.

While working for the government, he wrote a song, and began considering music as a career. At twenty-two, he left his job and entered the musical conservatory of St. Petersburg, Russia, where he studied composition and orchestration. Upon graduation from the conservatory, he moved to Moscow, and became an instructor of music theory at the Moscow Conservatory of music where he began composing.

Tchaikovsky completed his first symphony in 1868 (age twenty-eight) and his first opera a year later. Both were successful with Russian audiences. He also began writing music for ballets. In 1878, he married his wife, Antonina, but the marriage was a failure, and he soon left her.

After Tchaikovsky's marriage failed, a wealthy widow, Nadezhda von Meck, began supporting him financially. This enabled him to leave his teaching position and devote full-time to composing. It also allowed him to travel to the musical capitals of Europe. Madame von Meck supported Tchaikovsky for thirteen years on one condition: that he never attempt to meet her. For the first few years, Tchaikovsky composed much music, but from 1881 to 1888, he traveled extensively and wrote very little.

In 1888 (age forty-eight), the Russian government recognized Tchaikovsky's talents and gave him an annual salary for life. He then spent two years touring Europe as an orchestral conductor. In 1890, Madame von Meck ended her financial support. Although Tchaikovsky no longer needed the money, he was greatly hurt by this; he felt that his greatest supporter had abandoned him.

Tchaikovsky made an extended visit to the United States in 1891 (age fifty-one). He conducted an orchestral performance of one of his most famous works, the *1812 Overture*, at the grand opening of Carnegie Hall in New York City. He found the United States exciting, both musically and intellectually. When he returned to Russia, however, he was once again depressed over the loss of support from Madame von Meck. He died in St. Petersburg during a cholera epidemic.

Peter Ilyich Tchaikovsky was a handsome and vain man. He agonized over his music. He always had the feeling that it was never good enough and that the audience would not like it. He alternated between periods of writing and traveling. When he was writing he had a daily routine: he would work from 9:30 to 11:00 in the morning, have lunch, take a walk, and work again from 5:00 to 7:00 in the evening before dinner. Without financial support from others, Tchaikovsky might have spent his entire career as an instructor at the Moscow Conservatory.

Famous Works:

1812 Overture — for orchestra
Swan Lake — a ballet
Nutcracker — a ballet
Romeo and Juliet — an overture for orchestra
His six symphonies — for orchestra

"Oh, how difficult it is to make anyone see and feel in music what we see and feel ourselves."

Peter Ilyich Tchaikovsky, in a letter to his patron, Nadezhda von Meck

Ralph Vaughan Williams

His last name is "Vaughan Williams"— Vaughan (rhymes with "dawn") is not his middle name. He preferred that his first name be pronounced "Rayf."

born October 12, 1872, Down Ampney, England
died August 26, 1958, London, England

A Composer of the Twentieth Century

Ralph Vaughan Williams's father was a pastor who died when Ralph was three. Ralph and his mother then lived with his grandparents. As a child, he studied piano and violin. After graduating from a boys' school, Ralph enrolled at the Royal College of Music in London and married Adeline Fisher in 1897 (age twenty-five). He continued his education at Cambridge University, where he received his doctorate in music in 1901.

Vaughan Williams then took a job as a church organist in London. He performed the typical duties of a church organist: he accompanied services, rehearsed and directed the choir, and gave organ recitals. After three years, Vaughan Williams became restless, feeling that he should be doing something to contribute to the advancement of music, and of British music specifically. To fill this desire, he became interested in British folk music. He joined the Folk-Song Society, which collected and researched the songs and ballads which had been sung in Britain for centuries. Vaughan Williams arranged some of the newly collected folk songs for choirs.

Folk songs then became the basis for compositions which Vaughan Williams began to write. He quickly produced several orchestral and choral works based on English folk songs. It developed Vaughan Williams's interest in composing, but he was unsatisfied with his compositions and briefly gave up writing. He regained his interest and in 1908 (age thirty-six) he went to Paris to study with composer Maurice Ravel, even though Ravel was much younger than Vaughan Williams. His studies with Ravel, and his introduction to contemporary music in Paris, confirmed his desire to compose.

Between 1909 and the outbreak of World War I in 1914, Vaughan Williams completed several important works, including two symphonies. Although he was forty-two when the war began, Vaughan Williams enlisted in the military and saw service in Europe. After the war he became a professor at the Royal College of Music, where he taught composition. He was the typical studious professor, somewhat rumpled in appearance, though physically large and overbearing. In addition, he frequently conducted choral groups in London. For the rest of his long life, Vaughan Williams composed regularly, producing a large number of compositions, including symphonies, operas, ballets, songs, and choral works. He also wrote keyboard music and film scores.

Ralph Vaughan Williams's compositions were popular with audiences and music critics, and he was recognized during his lifetime as one of England's greatest musicians. In 1935 the British government awarded him the Order of Merit, a great honor given for distinguished service in art, literature, or science. His music always seemed to have a "British" style about it, even when it was not directly based on British folk songs. Vaughan Williams's first published work came when he was a student, at age nineteen. He finished his *Ninth Symphony* just before his death at age eighty-five. This sixty-six year span of creativity is one of the longest of any composer.

Famous Works:

His nine symphonies — for orchestra
Fantasia on a Theme by Thomas Tallis — for orchestra
Toward the Unknown Region — for chorus and orchestra
The Pilgrim's Progress — an opera
Job — a ballet

"In Vaughan Williams we hear the historic speech of the English people."

Hubert Foss, a publisher, reviewer, and composer

Giuseppe Verdi

Joo-sehp'-eh Vehr'-dee

born October 9 or 10, 1813, Le Roncole, Italy
died January 1, 1901, Milan, Italy

A Composer of the Romantic Era

Giuseppe Verdi's parents were innkeepers in the small town of Le Roncole, Italy. As a child, Giuseppe took organ lessons, and by age ten he was the village organist. His father sent him to live with a family friend in the nearby village of Busseto to study with the organist at the Busseto cathedral. After spending a few years studying in Milan, Italy, Verdi became conductor of the town orchestra in Busseto. He was married there in 1836.

At twenty-five, Verdi completed his first opera, *Oberto*, and moved back to Milan where the opera was performed. It was so successful that the opera manager commissioned three more operas from Verdi. While writing the first of the three operas, his wife and two children died. The opera was a failure. Verdi was very discouraged, but the opera manager convinced him to write the other two. He did, and both were successful.

Verdi then traveled to London, England, and Paris, France, and wrote an opera in each city. He was greatly influenced by the English and French styles of opera. His next successful operas were *Rigoletto* (1851), *Il Trovatore* (1853), and *La Traviata* (1853). The success of these operas made him Italy's most famous composer. His next seven operas, however, were not successful, yet he continued to improve as a composer.

By his mid-fifties, Verdi had developed a mature, traditionally Italian style for his operas. These works were big, lengthy operas with large casts of singers and large orchestras. Typical of this larger style was *Aida*, which was commissioned for a new opera house in Egypt to celebrate the opening of the Suez Canal. The premiere was delayed two years. There were problems with the libretto and it became impossible to transport the massive scenery because of war in Europe.

Aida was finally premiered in Cairo, Egypt, on Christmas Eve, 1871, with an audience from around the world. But Verdi did not attend; he disliked grand events and did not enjoy ocean travel.

The huge success of *Aida* made Italian audiences forget Verdi's unsuccessful operas. Now famous and wealthy, he married an opera singer, Giuseppina Strepponi. After *Aida* he wrote nothing for fifteen years; he began to feel that his operas were somewhat dated and he was not keeping up with what audiences wanted to hear. He and Giuseppina moved to a large farm he purchased with income from his opera performances.

He may never have written again except that he received a story for an opera from the Italian author Arrigo Boito based on *Othello* by William Shakespeare. Verdi composed an opera based on Boito's story (the story of an opera is called a libretto) and *Othello* was premiered, with much success, in 1887. Another opera based on Shakespeare, *Falstaff*, followed in 1893. Verdi was eighty years old when he completed *Falstaff*, and it would be his last work. He died eight years later. Giuseppe Verdi was a modest, confident composer who devoted his life to opera.

Famous Works:

Aida — an opera
Rigoletto — an opera
La Traviata — an opera
Falstaff — an opera
Il Trovatore — an opera

"In the theatre the public will stand for everything except boredom."

Giuseppe Verdi

Antonio Vivaldi

An-tohn'-ee-oh Vee-vahl'-dee

born March 4, 1678, Venice, Italy
died July 28, 1741, Vienna, Austria

A Composer of the Baroque Era

Antonio Vivaldi learned the craft of music from his father, a violinist in a church orchestra in Venice, Italy. Young Antonio served in church orchestras and eventually studied for the priesthood. He was ordained as a priest in 1703 at the age of twenty-five but never served the church in a religious capacity. However, he remained active in music, and served the church as a musician.

Vivaldi began composing sonatas for keyboard instruments around 1705. He also played violin in opera orchestras, developed a love of opera, and composed several operas. This was unusual and controversial; priests were not supposed to compose music for non-church related activities. His first opera was performed in 1713 (age thirty-five).

From 1709 through 1714, Vivaldi had the financial backing of an Italian prince in the city of Mantua, and he continued composing operas in addition to keyboard, vocal, and orchestral works. When the prince ended his support, Vivaldi accepted a position as orchestral conductor at St. Mark's Cathedral in Venice, Italy, the same church and orchestra in which his father had played violin. He held this position for twenty-seven years. He also served as the director of a musical conservatory in Venice.

By 1719 (age forty-one), another wealthy patron had begun to provide financial support for Vivaldi. For the next several years he composed operas for opera companies throughout Italy, including Rome and Milan, where audiences were the most discriminating. By 1725 his compositions, including his operas, were well known throughout Europe. His music was more popular in Holland, France, and England than in Italy; many Italians were uncomfortable with an ordained priest composing operas. In fact, in 1734, one of his operas was banned in Italy because he was a priest.

Vivaldi traveled throughout Europe in the late 1730s and early 1740s and lived briefly in Holland, where his music was very popular. Despite occasional disagreements with the church over his operas, Vivaldi remained as orchestral conductor at St. Mark's in Venice. In 1741 (age sixty-three), he moved to Vienna, Austria, hoping to receive an offer as a court musician or composer. However, he received no offers and died in Vienna.

After Vivaldi's death, his music was rarely performed until the twentieth century, when musicians and audiences rediscovered it. During his lifetime, he was known as an opera composer. Today, while his operas are again being performed, his orchestral works are most popular. Vivaldi claimed to have written ninety-four operas but musical scholars have found scores for only fifty.

Antonio Vivaldi was a pleasant man with a full head of bright red hair. For this he was sometimes referred to as "the red priest." He was comfortable writing music for both religious and concert performances.

Famous Works:

The Four Seasons — a set of four concertos for violin and orchestra
Concerto Grosso in D minor — for two violins, cello, and string orchestra
His concertos for various instruments and orchestra
His masses, and sacred choral works
His operas

"I heard him undertake to compose a concerto, with all the parts, with greater dispatch than a copyist can copy it."

Charles de Brosses, French historian, describing Antonio Vivaldi

Richard Wagner

Rikh'-art Vahg'-ner

born May 22, 1813, Leipzig Germany
died February 13, 1883, Venice, Italy

A Composer of the Romantic Era

Richard Wagner was the youngest of nine children. After his father died and his mother remarried, Richard was raised by his stepfather, an actor and painter. Richard attended good schools, but as a child he was not particularly interested in music.

At sixteen he entered the university in Leipzig, Germany, where he developed an interest in music and began studying it seriously. Between the ages of nineteen and twenty-four, Wagner conducted several opera and theatrical companies, and began to compose operas. In every case, the opera companies failed or Wagner was fired. He was not a reliable employee, and was always in debt because he lived beyond his means. He married Minna Planer, an actress, in 1836 (age twenty-one). She died in 1861 and Wagner then married Cosima Liszt, daughter of the composer Franz Liszt.

Wagner moved to Paris at twenty-four, hoping to achieve success as an opera composer, but again he failed. Some of his operas were performed but none successfully. In 1842 (age twenty-seven), he returned to Germany where his opera *Rienzi* was performed in Dresden. It was a success. Finally Wagner began to earn some income as well as the freedom to devote all his time to composing operas.

Unlike most opera composers, Wagner wrote both the libretto (the story of the opera) and the music. He based most of his librettos on German myths and legends. In 1849 (age thirty-four), he moved to Zurich, Switzerland. During the next fifteen years, he wrote essays and books on the subject of theatre and drama, poetry, as well as four operas. By 1860 (age forty-five), Wagner was producing his operas with his own money. Usually the performances were poorly received and lost money.

In 1864, Wagner received the financial support of a patron, King Ludwig II of Bavaria (today a part of Germany). Gradually, audiences began to support his operas. During this period, Wagner developed grand ideas about writing lengthy operas. His opera *Das Rheingold*, premiered in 1869, was the first of his grand operas. In 1876 (age sixty-three), he convinced King Ludwig and other patrons of the arts to build a lavish opera house in Bayreuth, Bavaria, for performances of his operas.

By this time Wagner thought of himself as a very important person in the opera world. He created "Wagner societies," a kind of fan club, to help pay for performances of his operas at Bayreuth. The Bayreuth theatre opened on August 13, 1876, with a complete performance of his cycle of four operas known as *The Ring of the Nibelung*. He composed only one more opera, *Parsifal*, before he died while on vacation in Venice, Italy.

Richard Wagner was vain, ambitious, egotistical, and, some would say, obnoxious. He had few friends. His first love was literature, and throughout his life he kept a notebook in which he wrote down every detail of his life.

Famous Works:

Tannhäuser — an opera
Tristan and Isolde — an opera
Lohengrin — an opera
Der Ring de Nibelungen (The Ring of the Nibelung) — an opera
Parsifal — an opera

"Melody is the absolute language in which the musician speaks to every heart."

Richard Wagner

About the Eras of Musical Style

Medieval Era (450–1450)

The period from approximately 450 through 1450 is known as the Middle Ages or the Medieval *(mee-dee'-vul)* era. Although some instrumental music was performed during this era, most Medieval music was vocal. This vocal music was of two types: sacred (music performed in churches) and secular (music performed outside the church). The sacred music was in a more formal style and the secular music was folk-like.

Secular music was the popular music of its time. It was frequently performed by traveling musicians who sang ballads and accompanied themselves on stringed and percussion instruments. Common stringed instruments were small harps, lutes (which developed into today's guitar), and viols (bowed string instruments which developed into today's violin). Percussion instruments included drums, cymbals, and bells. Wind instruments such as flutes and bagpipes were also played.

The music of the church, primarily the Roman Catholic Church, is very important in the history and development of music. For centuries, beginning in the Medieval era, the church was the primary place where serious musicians could perform music together.

Through about 1150, church music consisted mostly of a single melody sung by one person or a group. The singers were almost always men. The music of Hildegard von Bingen is an exception; her music was sung almost exclusively by women.

Instead of speaking a prayer, a priest would sing it on various pitches. These "prayers sung on pitches" are called chants. Priests would make up the chants and teach them to other priests or male singers. It's the same way you first learned songs in school. Your music teacher sang a song and you sang it after him or her. After singing it a few times, you could remember the entire song and sing it by yourself or in a group.

As more and more prayers were set to chants, it became difficult for priests and singers to remember them all. So singers developed a group of written symbols, called neumes (pronounced *nooms*). The first neume, a black square, indicated the starting point. Other neumes and symbols indicated whether the next note was higher or lower. It looked more like a graph than today's musical symbols. Neumes were the first music notation. They weren't exact, but they allowed singers to sing many more chants than they could memorize.

Eventually horizontal lines were added and the neumes were placed on the lines. The horizontal lines developed into the musical staff we use today, and the neumes developed into notes.

During the period 900-1200, singers began to add a second part to the single-line chants. Music with more than one voice part is called polyphony. In the Medieval era the second melody was usually below the original melody by an interval of a fourth or fifth. The two parts moved together rhythmically and melodically. This is called parallel movement. A chant with a second, lower, parallel part is called organum. (This name has nothing to do with an organ.) Ask your music teacher to play a melody with a parallel melody a fourth or fifth below to hear how organum sounds.

The growth of polyphony continued through the last 300 years of the Medieval era (1150-1450). Neumes developed into more formalized notation, and this allowed music to be more carefully planned by composers. By 1400 the first great cathedrals were being built in Europe, giving composers wonderful places for their music to be performed. Remember, virtually all the serious music written in the Medieval era was sacred vocal music.

Some Composers of the Medieval Era

Hildegard von Bingen (1098–1179)

Guillaume de Machaut (1300–1377)

John Dunstable (1385–1453)

Guillaume Dufay (1400–1474)

Renaissance Era (1450–1600)

The term Renaissance is used to describe not only music but all the arts and architecture during the period 1450-1600. The word "renaissance" means rebirth or revival, and the term was originally used to mean a revival of the study of the classical Greek and Roman eras. Architects, for example, began to design buildings in ancient Greek and Roman styles. In music, however, the term Renaissance is used simply because it corresponds with this era in the arts.

In the Renaissance era, as in the Medieval era (450-1450), vocal music was more important than instrumental music, and sacred music was more important than secular (non-sacred) music. Polyphony (music with more than one voice part) continued to develop. In the Medieval era, two vocal parts were usually sung in parallel. In the Renaissance era, those two vocal parts were more likely to sing independently of each other. Two or more voices singing independently is called counterpoint.

Composers now began to write music for three, four, five, or even more voice parts. All the parts were equally important. In other words, one voice was not assigned to sing the melody while the other voices harmonized. Every voice part sang its own melody, and no melody was any more or less important than the others.

By the end of the Medieval era, composers began to set the entire Roman Catholic Mass to chants. Renaissance composers continued this practice, and the Mass became one of the main forms of vocal music. Another was the motet, an unaccompanied vocal work based on a sacred Latin text.

Sometimes, a vocal mass had an instrumental accompaniment, although the instruments had not developed much since the Medieval era. Renaissance era instruments included plucked string instruments like the lute, bowed string instruments like the viol, and flutes, recorders, and horns. Usually the instruments simply played the same parts as the voices. When an instrument plays the same line as a vocal part, the instrument is said to be doubling the vocal part.

The written notation of the Medieval era developed into a system of lines and spaces that began to look like today's musical staff, clefs, and notes. This allowed composers to write music that was more complicated and sophisticated.

Great cathedrals continued to be built in Europe, and most of these large churches now contained organs. The organ, therefore, became the primary keyboard instrument. Another popular keyboard instrument was the harpsichord. A harpsichord resembles a piano but on a harpsichord the strings are plucked when the player strikes a key. On a piano the strings are struck, with a small hammer, when a key is depressed. A harpsichord cannot play as loudly as a piano.

By the beginning of the Renaissance era, most European royalty hired musicians to perform and entertain at special events. Traveling musicians continued to perform secular music for average citizens. The primary secular music form of the Renaissance era was the madrigal. A madrigal is a type of vocal music usually set to a poem. The goal of the composer is to enhance the meaning of the poem with music.

Sacred music, however, was still the dominant type of music throughout the Renaissance era.

Some Composers of the Renaissance Era

Josquin des Prez (1450–1521)

Giovanni da Palestrina (1525–1594)

William Byrd (1543–1623)

Giulio Caccini (1546–1618)

Luca Marenzio (1553–1599)

Giovanni Gabrielli (1557–1612)

Thomas Morley (1557–1602)

Claudio Monteverdi (1567–1643)

Baroque Era (1600–1750)

The term "baroque," meaning an extravagant style, was originally applied to the architecture of the period 1600-1750. But like the term Renaissance, the term Baroque is used to define a period of music.

In the Renaissance era (1450–1600), vocal music was the dominant type of music. While sacred vocal music continued to develop in the Baroque era, both secular (non-sacred) and instrumental music became much more important. In fact, the Baroque era was the first period in which instrumental music was as important as vocal music.

In the polyphonic music of the Renaissance era, all of the voice parts were equally important. In the Baroque era, one voice, usually the highest voice part (the soprano voice), was given the melody while the other lower voices harmonized the melody. So the soprano voice part became the most important part because it sang the melody. Polyphonic music continued to develop, in both vocal and instrumental music.

In the Renaissance era, a piece of music sounded pretty much the same from start to finish. But in the Baroque era, composers began to write contrasting sections within a piece. A slow section (or movement) would follow a fast section. Or a soft section would follow a loud one. The best example of this is the sonata, a new musical form developed in the Baroque era. A sonata is an instrumental work for a solo instrument performing alone or with accompaniment, in three contrasting movements, such as fast-slow-fast or loud-soft-loud.

Other new musical forms included cantatas and oratorios, multi-movement vocal works with instrumental accompaniment. Oratorios were more likely to be sacred, and were frequently based on the Bible. Cantatas could be sacred or secular. Neither cantatas nor oratorios used staging, scenery, or costumes.

The opera, which did use staging, scenery, costumes, and action, also developed during the Baroque era. An opera is a play, usually secular, set to music and staged, with orchestral accompaniment.

When instruments accompanied singers in the Renaissance era, they usually doubled the voices. But in the Baroque era, the instruments which accompanied singers in oratorios, cantatas, and operas had their own parts—they truly accompanied the singers.

The orchestras which accompanied singers in the Baroque era were different from today's orchestras. Today the instruments of the orchestra are established by centuries of tradition. A composer writing for orchestra knows what instruments will be available. In the Baroque era, however, an "orchestra" was likely to be whatever musicians were available at the time. Eventually, composers began to specify which instruments should play which parts. This began the development of the modern orchestra.

The instruments were developing, too. The viols of the Renaissance era became violins, violas, cellos, and bass violins. Flutes and oboes became more like today's instruments, and around 1700, the first clarinets were used. Trombones were similar to today's instruments, but trumpets had no valves and were difficult to play. Some had slides, like miniature trombones! Music notation in the Baroque era looked pretty much as it does today.

In previous eras, music was written for specific purposes, most often as part of a church service. During the Baroque era, music became more expressive. For the first time, people went to vocal and orchestral concerts for the sole purpose of hearing the music.

Some Composers of the Baroque Era

Claudio Monteverdi (1567–1643)

Jean-Baptist Lully (1632–1687)

Arcangelo Corelli (1653–1713)

Henry Purcell (1659–1695)

Antonio Vivaldi (1678–1741)

George Frideric Handel (1685–1759)

Johann Sebastian Bach (1685–1750)

Domenico Scarlatti (1685–1757)

Giovanni Pergolesi (1710–1736)

Classical Era (1750–1825)

The term "classical" is used in different ways. When some people refer to "classical" music, they mean "serious" music, as opposed to popular or folk music. But when musicians use the term "classical music," they mean music written between 1750 and 1825.

The music of this era can best be described as elegant, formal, and restrained. For the first time, instrumental music was more important than vocal music. In fact, the most important new musical form of the Classical era was the symphony, an extended work in several movements (often four) for orchestra.

The symphony grew out of the sonata, a popular form of the Baroque era. A sonata is a work for solo instrument, either alone or accompanied. In a symphony, there is no solo instrument, and the orchestra becomes the "instrument" for the composer. So a symphony could be described as a sonata for orchestra.

Another Classical era form which evolved from the sonata is the concerto. A concerto is a sonata for a solo instrument, accompanied by an orchestra.

The Classical era orchestra was very similar to today's orchestra, though smaller in size. The instruments were basically the same as those in a modern orchestra. The string instruments were identical to today's violins, violas, cellos, and string basses. The string section was the most important part of the Classical era orchestra. Woodwind and brass instruments had also evolved and were similar to today's flutes, oboes, clarinets, horns, trumpets, and trombones. Percussion instruments included drums, cymbals, and timpani.

The organ was still an important instrument. But the piano replaced the harpsichord as the most popular keyboard instrument. The piano could play louder than a harpsichord and thus could produce sounds from very loud to very soft. Musicians call this a wide dynamic range. The piano's wide dynamic range made it appealing to Classical era composers.

In the Baroque era, musical works had contrasting sections, such as fast-slow-fast, or loud-soft-loud. There were no changes in tempo or loudness (what musicians call the dynamic level) within a section. It was fast, or loud, the whole way through. In the Classical era, composers began to change the tempo or the dynamic level within a section. The changes could be gradual or sudden. A movement could begin slowly and gradually increase in tempo. Or a soft section might suddenly become loud.

The vocal forms of the Baroque era, such as operas, oratorios, and cantatas remained popular with Classical era composers.

Many composers of the Classical era were employed or supported by European royalty or aristocrats. This type of employment is called patronage. The aristocrat was a patron of the composer. He commissioned compositions from the composer and paid him for his musical creations. This gave the composer a continuing source of income, an outlet for his music, and the freedom to develop his craft. Composers of the Classical era could best be described as fine musical craftsmen.

Many composers traveled throughout Europe to perform their music and to hear the music of other composers. This resulted in a single style for music of the Classical era—a style that is elegant and formal, and which sounded the same in Rome, Italy, as it did in Vienna, Austria.

Some Composers of the Classical Era

Christoph Gluck (1714–1787)

Franz Joseph Haydn (1732–1809)

Johann Christian Bach (1735–1782)

Wolfgang Amadeus Mozart (1756–1791)

Ludwig van Beethoven (1770–1827)

Carl Maria von Weber (1786–1826)

Gioacchino Rossini (1792–1868)

Franz Schubert (1797–1828)

Romantic Era (1825–1900)

The term Romantic, when applied to this era (1825–1900), pertains to music with an imaginative emotional appeal. Romantic era music emphasizes personal feelings and emotions. Composers who wrote during this period wanted to express their innermost thoughts and feelings through their music.

The emotional music of the Romantic era greatly contrasts with the music of the Classical era, which can best be described as elegant, formal, and restrained. Classical composers wrote very structured music. Romantic era composers were much more free with their music, using it to express themselves. The music of the Classical era sounded essentially the same throughout Europe. But Romantic era composers began to compose in nationalistic styles as a way to show their patriotism and love of country. For example, a German composer might use German folk tales as the basis for his music, or a Russian composer might incorporate Russian folk music in his compositions.

Composers were not only more free musically, they were also more free as individuals. Many, though certainly not all, were celebrities, like today's rock stars. Some were quite wealthy. A composer might earn income from the sale of printed copies of his music, or he might tour as a conductor throughout Europe and North America. Or he might produce performances of his music or operas, like today's concert promoters. Others were supported by wealthy patrons and a few were supported by their governments.

Music in the Romantic era frequently represented something (such as an element of nature, like a sunrise), or expressed something (such as love of country or patriotism), or described something (such as a poem). The orchestra truly became the composer's "instrument" during this era. Orchestras grew in size, and the skill of orchestration (scoring music for the various instruments of the orchestra) became an important part of the composer's craft. Composers began to use the instruments of the orchestra in much the same way that an artist uses colors—for effect, contrast, and beauty.

Great conservatories (schools which trained musicians) grew during the Romantic era, and this resulted in many more skilled performers than in previous eras. As orchestras employed more skilled performers, composers were able to write music that was more difficult.

New forms developed. The symphonic poem was a fairly long (as long as an hour) work for orchestra in one movement. Often a symphonic poem attempted to tell a story or paint a musical picture. Descriptive music such as this is called program music. Not all the new forms were orchestral. Composers also wrote short piano pieces, and songs for solo voice with piano accompaniment using expressive poems as the song lyrics. German composers, in particular, excelled at composing songs.

Perhaps the most grandiose new form of the Romantic era was the music drama, a kind of grandiose opera using an enormous cast and a large orchestra. The operas of Richard Wagner and Giuseppe Verdi were the best examples of music drama. Both Wagner and Verdi considered their operas to be a kind of super-art, combining music, drama, theater, and the visual arts of scenery and costuming.

By 1900, the great, emotional music of the Romantic era gave way to the composers of the twentieth century, who looked at music, and the art of composing, much differently than their predecessors in the nineteenth century.

Some Composers of the Romantic Era

Hector Berlioz (1803–1869)

Fanny Mendelssohn Hensel (1805–1847)

Felix Mendelssohn (1809–1847)

Frédéric Chopin (1810–1849)

Robert Schumann (1810–1856)

Franz Liszt (1811–1886)

Richard Wagner (1813–1883)

Giuseppe Verdi (1813–1901)

Clara Schumann (1819–1896)

César Franck (1822–1890)

Anton Bruckner (1824–1869)

Johannes Brahms (1833–1897)

Modest Mussorgsky (1839–1881)

Peter Ilyich Tchaikovsky (1840–1893)

Antonín Dvořák (1841–1904)

Edvard Grieg (1843–1907)

John Philip Sousa (1854–1932)

Edward Elgar (1857–1934)

Giacomo Puccini (1858–1924)

Gustav Mahler (1860–1911)

Claude Debussy (1862–1918)

Richard Strauss (1864–1949)

The Twentieth Century (1900–2000)

The Romantic era didn't suddenly end in 1900. The years 1890-1910, sometimes called the Post-Romantic era, were a musical transition period from the Romantic era into the twentieth century. During these two decades, a style of music known as Impressionism was popular. Impressionism took its name from artists who, instead of using clear lines to paint their pictures, used soft images to convey the impression of a scene. Impressionist composers did the same with music. They used new harmonies, chords, and melodies based on unfamiliar scales or modes to paint a soft musical picture, much like the program music of the Romantic era.

The main contribution of Impressionist music was the use of new musical harmonies and scales. These harmonies and scales allowed later twentieth century composers to develop music which was more complex and less rooted in traditional harmonies and melodies. The first style of twentieth century music which evolved from Impressionism was known as Neoclassicism, or New Classicism.

Neoclassicism was a return to musical elements of earlier eras of music, particularly the Baroque and Classical eras. These musical elements became the basis for new compositions using new harmonies, melodies, and rhythms. Neoclassic composers used strict forms, like Classical era composers, and much counterpoint, like Baroque era composers. Many composers, such as Igor Stravinsky and Aaron Copland wrote in this style well into the twentieth century.

After Impressionism, most composers abandoned the emotionalism and program music of the Romantic era and returned to the Classical era concept of music for its own sake. Other styles which developed in the twentieth century, include:

- Aleatory music or chance music — Music which is either composed or performed by chance procedures, such as rolling dice, or flipping a coin. Aleatory music will sound differently each time it is performed. In fact, it is not possible to predict exactly how it will sound!
- Serial music — Music based on a series of pitches, or rhythms, or any musical elements, which are repeated again and again. Twelve-tone music is a type of serial music which uses all twelve tones in the musical scale before repeating another, then repeating those tones in the same order over and over. Serial music can be aleatory music; the tones can be determined by chance.
- Atonal music — Music without a tonal center. From 1700 through 1900, virtually all serious music was written with a tonal center, or musical key. Because this music had what could be called a tonal center, it was known as tonal music. Atonal music has no key or tonal center, and the music can be quite dissonant. Serial music is usually atonal.
- Electronic music — Music created by electronic devices such as a synthesizer. Music created electronically allows the composer (as opposed to performers or a conductor) to control every aspect of the musical performance.

Instrumental music remained more influential than choral music throughout this era. Twentieth century music varies greatly; there is no single unifying style. Nevertheless, several stylistic elements are common to much twentieth century music. Rhythm and counterpoint became extremely important while melodies became less "singable." Harmony developed to the point of dissonance. And jazz, the dominant form of popular music for the first half of the century, influenced many composers.

Some Composers of the Twentieth Century

Scott Joplin (1868–1917)

Ralph Vaughan Williams (1872–1958)

Sergei Rachmaninov (1873–1943)

Arnold Schoenberg (1874–1951)

Charles Ives (1874–1954)

Maurice Ravel (1875–1937)

Béla Bartók (1881–1945)

Igor Stravinsky (1882–1971)

Sergei Prokofiev (1891–1953)

Francis Poulenc (1899–1963)

Duke Ellington (1899–1974)

George Gershwin (1898–1937)

Aaron Copland (1900–1990)

Dmitri Shostakovich (1906–1975)

Benjamin Britten (1913–1976)

Leonard Bernstein (1918–1990)

About the Author

Jay Althouse received a B.S. degree in Music Education and an M.Ed. degree in Music from Indiana University of Pennsylvania. For eight years he served as a rights and licenses administrator for a major educational music publisher. During that time he served a term on the Executive Board of the Music Publishers Association of America.

As a composer of sacred and secular choral music, Mr. Althouse has more than 600 works in print for choirs of all levels. His music is widely performed throughout the English-speaking world. He is a writer member of ASCAP and is a regular recipient of the ASCAP Special Award for his compositions in the area of standard music.

Mr. Althouse has also co-written several cantatas, songbooks, and musicals with his wife, Sally K. Albrecht, compiled and arranged a number of highly regarded vocal solo collections, and is the co-writer, of the best-selling books *The Complete Choral Warm-up Book*, and *Accent on Composers*, a reproducible sourcebook for classroom music teachers featuring the music and lives of 22 composers. His most recent books are *Ready to Read Music*, a music reading readiness book for young students, and *Sixty Music Quizzes*, a supplemental book of music quizzes. He is the co-writer, with Sally K. Albrecht, of *I Hear America Singing!*, a choral work performed at the Inauguration of President Barack Obama on January 20, 2009.

Other Reproducible Books from Alfred

Accent on Composers

The Music and Lives of 22 Great Composers, with Listening CD, Review/Tests, and Supplemental Materials

Jay Althouse and Judith O'Reilly

Introduce students to the lives and music of 22 great composers with this 100% reproducible book, complete with listening CD. Students will study the life of the composer, then listen to a well-known, representative musical work. Includes quizzes and answer keys. Recommended for grades 6 and up.

CD KIT: Teacher's Reproducible Handbook/CD 00-20048

Ready to Read Music

Sequential Lessons in Music Reading Readiness

Jay Althouse

Don't ask your students to read music until they are "ready to read music." This 100% reproducible book is packed with four sequential units of eight lessons each, all designed to prepare your students to read music. As a bonus, there are pages of large reproducible music symbols. Recommended for K–8.

Reproducible Book 00-21835

Please visit **alfred.com** for more information on these and other Alfred classroom resources.

All Alfred materials are available from your favorite music dealer.

Alfred Music Publishing Co., Inc.
16320 Roscoe Blvd., Suite 100
P.O. Box 10003
Van Nuys, CA 91410-0003

alfred.com

60 Music Quizzes for Theory and Reading

One-page Reproducible Tests to Evaluate Student Musical Skills

Jay Althouse

Just what the title says: 60 one-page quizzes on a variety of subjects related to beginning music theory and reading. Perfect for student assessment. Includes answer keys. Recommended for grades 3 and up.

Reproducible Book 00-27144

Music Fun 101

101 Reproducible Music Games and Puzzles

Sue Albrecht Johnson

This incredible publication includes all your favorite games and puzzles, from Alphagrams, Matching Puzzles, and Crosswords to Name That Tune, Musical Sudokus, Word Searches, Mazes, and more! Clever, educational, reproducible, and fantastic fun for everyone. Includes answer keys. Recommended for grades 3 and up.

Reproducible Book 00-28861

Music Puzzles Plus

25 Educational and Fun Puzzles for Classroom and Home Use

Donald Moore

Music Puzzles Plus includes 25 music games and puzzles designed to make music learning fun and easy. Included are Word Searches, Rounders, "Name That Tune" games, Word Puzzles, Geography Puzzles, and Crossword Puzzles. Answer keys are included. Recommended for grades 5 and up.

Reproducible Book 00-23857